THRIVING IN
TROUBLED
TIMES

THRIVING IN TROUBLED TIMES

Meeting God in the Middle of Our Mess

BY BARNEY CARGILE III

DEDICATION

This book is dedicated to my two children, Josh and Tiffany. I have learned far more from them than they could ever possibly learn from me.

ACKNOWLEDGMENTS

I want to acknowledge four ladies who made this book possible. Thank you, Fallon Sealund, for your technical skills and for enduring my endless array of questions. To my editor, Christi McGuire, thank you for your encouragement, expertise, and speedy work. A special thanks to Denise Loock, who edited my first book, *Thriving in Quarantine*, and encouraged me to write *Thriving in Troubled Times*. And of course my wife, Linda, who continues to be my greatest source of inspiration.

CONTENTS

Part Three: Hope & Reality

Part Four: Gratitude

PREFACE

My first book, *Thriving in Quarantine*, chronicled our family's adventures aboard the *Grand Princess*. When COVID-19 was discovered onboard, we were confined to our quarters for six days and then quarantined at Travis Air Force Base in California for two weeks.

We returned home, only to discover the whole world was in quarantine. Like everyone else, we expected life to return to "normal" after a few weeks. But, as Patsy Clairmont suggests, "Normal is just a setting on your dryer." "Normal" hasn't returned and perhaps won't.

The nonprofit I worked for, Crossing the Jordan, closed down, ending that chapter of my life. I was heartbroken. Our retail store, The Bird's Nest, appeared destined for the same fate, but God supernaturally intervened and saved it. He's given us multiple signs that we are to stay open and remain in California. Now we face the same situation as on the ship—wrestling with periods of anxiety and uncertainty. But God continues to pour His grace on us.

People are hurting, overwhelmed with fear. Witnessing this, I sat down to write, and *Thriving in Troubled Times* emerged. In *Thriving in Quarantine*, I described four spiritual practices that carried us though our struggles: Trusting God, Joy in the Moment, Hope, and Gratitude. I've drawn from those same four practices to create four sections in *Thriving in Troubled Times*. Just as God empowered us, not only to survive our shipboard trauma but also to thrive in quarantine, He continues to empower us to thrive in troubled times. My prayer is that these fifty meditations will inspire you to do exactly that.

INTRODUCTION

He's an unwelcome house guest, but he knocks often on the door of our lives. He can show up anytime... but he especially loves to interrupt our nocturnal rest. He's a persistent pest who perpetually pounds on our entryway. If we make the mistake of opening the door of our minds, he quickly slides through, scurries across the floor, and settles into an easy chair. Only then do we notice he's not alone. That pest Anxiety has dragged in his family—Worry, Fear, Doubt, and Stress, along with a few other reprehensible relatives.

Anxiety *will* knock on our door. That's a given. When we face uncertainty, without fail he comes calling. But we always have a choice. We don't need to open the door. And we certainly don't have to set the table and serve him dinner. Nor do we need to allow Anxiety and his family to settle in for the night. And we definitely don't have any obligation to give them a place in our beds.

Anxiety, worry, and fear arguably create more health issues than any other cause. They often lie at the root of heart problems, digestive troubles, and nervous conditions. And that's not even considering the toll they can take on relationships.

It doesn't require a PhD in social science to realize we are living in anxious, fearful times. Politics, pandemics, wars, the environment, economics, natural disasters. Add to that the day-to-day concerns over our families, health, and personal finances. Turn on the evening news (if you dare) and make note of all the troubles in our world. When we retire for the night, I'm confident those newsworthy stories will visit our dreams in unpleasant ways.

We can't avoid the anxieties of twenty-first century living, nor do we need binoculars to seek out anxiety. It interrupts our days, tapping us on the shoulder and demanding our attention, even knocking on our doors at night. At times we may wonder if there's anywhere we can turn for help.

That's the bad news. But there's always more good news than bad news. God is in charge of the universe. That's good news. Jesus has not abandoned us. More good news. He has given us the Holy Spirit who lives in us as our Comforter. That's the "best good news" of all.

God has equipped us with all the tools we need to ward off this blight of anxiety and fear. We have His promises in Scripture. He's available 24/7/365 to cast our concerns upon. The peace of the Holy Spirit is just a prayer away.

In some small way, my desire is for this devotional book to bring relief when anxiety plagues our minds. It includes fifty short readings, each containing a story (usually humorous), Scripture, and an application. Each reading also contains a *Principle* (or truth), a *Promise* from God's Word, questions to *Ponder*, a *Prayer* to offer strength, a Scripture to *Pursue* deeper, and *Perceptions* to journal, draw, or meditate upon.

Many of these were birthed from my own personal struggles with anxiety, especially within the past few months. My prayer is you will be blessed and encouraged by each of these devotionals. May we all step into the abundant life Jesus intended for each of us.

TRUSTING GOD

"May everyone who knows your mercy keep putting
their trust in you, for they can count on you for help
no matter what. O Lord, you will never, no never,
neglect those who come to you." (Psalm 9:10 TPT)

"Trusting God's plan is the only secret I know
in the gentle art of not freaking out."
(Lysa TerKeurst)

MY 13,000-FOOT LEAP OF FAITH

I crouched at the edge of the door, my heels firmly resting on the plane's floor. My toes pointed toward terra firma, 13,000 feet below. For a split second I considered turning back. But it was too late. With my instructor firmly strapped to my back, I pushed off.

The air blasted my face as if I'd stuck my head out of a car window at 100 mph. I gasped for breath, wondering, "Will the parachute open?" After a minute of free fall, it unfolded. For the next five minutes, I peacefully drifted over the vineyards of Central California. My senses feasted on the experience. Eventually, my instructor guided us to a gentle landing. I had literally taken a leap of faith, having no choice but to entrust my life to him. Having successfully completed 14,000 jumps, he was easy to trust. My mind could rest knowing I was in safe hands.

At times God calls us to take a leap of faith, even when we are unsure of where He's leading us. We trust Him to catch us as we take the plunge, just as I trusted my instructor. It may be a career change, moving our family, or standing on our integrity. Hebrews 11:1 explains,

"Faith means being sure of the things we hope for and knowing that something is real even if we do not see it" (NCV). The verses that follow supply us with a plethora of examples from Noah, Abraham, Sarah, Moses, Joshua, and Rahab. Ordinary people with extraordinary trust.

Is taking a leap of faith stressful and anxiety-ridden? You bet. Trusting God as we fall is downright scary, I know. But the alternative of *not* trusting God is unthinkable. Traveling through life, we're going to experience lots of troubles (John 16:33). We can either face them *with* God or *without* Him. Which one's more stressful? Hmm. Let me think.

It comes down to how much we trust our Instructor. Jesus told His followers, "Put your trust in Me" (John 14:1 NLV). Maybe Jesus didn't make 14,000 skydiving jumps, but He took the ultimate leap when He came to earth. His credentials are far greater than any human's. He's the all-powerful, all-seeing, all-knowing Creator. Let's strap ourselves securely to Him and take that leap of faith. He'll guide you all the way to safety.

Principle: We can trust Jesus, our Instructor, when He calls us to take a leap of faith.

Promise: Jesus will guide us all the way to safety.

Ponder:

- After reading Hebrews 11, which example do you most relate to?
- In what specific area do you need to trust God and take a leap of faith?

Prayer: *Lord, increase my faith, so that I'm willing to totally trust You with every area of my life.*

Pursue: For a deeper dive, study Hebrews chapter 11.

Perceptions: Record any ideas God puts on your heart from this devotion.

MONUMENT TO A BOLL WEEVIL

In Enterprise, Alabama, a peculiar monument rises thirteen feet above the town square. A statue of a woman stands atop a marble pillar, holding a pedestal overhead that supports (of all things) a gigantic bronze boll weevil. But the story possesses an even more bizarre twist. Each October the community hosts a Boll Weevil Festival, honoring this pesky insect. Much as Santa Claus arriving in the Macy's Thanksgiving Day Parade, the festival highlights a giant attired weevil dancing down the street. Locals even compete in a boll weevil costume contest. Why is such an honor bestowed on a creature known for its destruction?

In the early 1900s, cotton farming was the mainstay for the local economy. But over time, boll weevils decimated their crops. Realizing their livelihood was in jeopardy, the farmers diversified, planting new crops such as soybeans. In the process, they discovered a sweet serendipity. These new crops actually created greater profitability for the farmers, delivering them from economic ruin. The boll weevils turned out to be a blessing in disguise. So the monument's plaque reads,

4

"In appreciation of the Boll Weevil and what it has done as the Herald of Prosperity..."

That certainly flips things on its head! What had been viewed as a curse turned out to be a blessing. It's a powerful testimony to one of the most popular and profound promises in Scripture. Romans 8:28 declares, "All things work together for good to those who love God" (NKJV). Notice that it doesn't say "all things are good." Rather, God promises to bring good out of every struggle we face—to turn our greatest tragedies into our greatest triumphs.

Scripture demonstrates this repeatedly. Just start reading Genesis. Noah, Abraham, Joseph...the list goes on and on about how God turned tragedies into triumphs. Most profoundly, we witness this truth at the cross. God took the worst tragedy in history and transformed it into the greatest triumph that ever occurred—the salvation of the human race!

Napoleon Hill wrote, "Every adversity brings with it the seed of an equal advantage."[1] Is it possible that the painful experiences we encounter hold seeds of even greater blessings? Rather than despairing over our "boll weevils," those stressful, anxious situations we view as the bane of our existence, why not embrace them? Our greatest disasters could turn out to be our greatest blessings.

---

[1]   Napoleon Hill, *Think and Grow Rich!* (Wise, VA: The Napoleon Hill Foundation, 2017).

Principle: Our greatest disasters could turn out to be our greatest blessings.

Promise: "All things work together for good to those who love God." (Romans 8:28)

Ponder:

- What "boll weevils" (anxious and stressful situations) are you currently experiencing?
- How can you view these as potential blessings?

Prayer: *Loving Father, I trust You and believe You always want what's best for me. Help me embrace the "boll weevils" that come my way and look for the "seeds of blessings" they contain.*

Pursue: For a deeper dive, study Daniel 6, as an example of Romans 8:28.

Perceptions: Record any ideas God puts on your heart from this devotion.

GOD IS FOR US

When my son, Josh, was eight, he was hit in the nose with a baseball bat. He was playing ball with some boys, and one of them clobbered him on the backswing. We rushed him to the ER and were immediately ushered in. Besides a broken nose, Josh was sporting a nasty gash between his eyes, requiring multiple stitches. You can imagine, as an eight-year-old, Josh thrashed about in agony. The doctor needed someone to hold his flailing head and arms in place, and Yours Truly was elected.

As I stood directly over him, pinning his arms down and firmly securing his head in place, the doctor injected a numbing agent into Josh's cut, which must have been torturous. I'll never forget the look on my son's face. His expression screamed, "Why, Dad? Why are you letting him hurt me? How could a loving father subject me to such torment?" Of course we know the answer. I did it to help him. I was actually loving him...only it didn't feel like love to Josh. Afterward, Linda and I collapsed into each other's arms, weeping over our son's pain.

It's the same with God. As a loving Father, He allows us to experience pain. Human suffering is too deep to understand, but here's my take on it. I don't believe God causes bad things to happen to us. Our own foolish choices, the circumstances of life, and the Enemy create the tragedies we experience. (See the book of Job). But at times God permits tragedies, without stepping in to stop our pain. Often, He "holds our head in place" as we scream, "Why, God? How could a loving Father let this happen?" The answer is the same as my experience with Josh. At that particular point, God is right there with us, weeping with us, loving us—in ways that may not feel like love.

In this life we're not capable of comprehending the "why." It's simply too deep for us to grasp. But in the midst of pain, grab hold of this indisputable fact: *God is for you!* Romans 8 promises: "If God is for us, who can be against us?" (v. 31) and "nothing in all creation will ever be able to separate us from the love of God" (v. 39 NLT). Amazing! We're not capable of understanding God's actions, but we trust Him—no matter how deep the pain...because God is for you!

Principle: God is for us.

Promise: Nothing can separate us from God's love.

Ponder:

- When have you felt God was not with you, only to later discover He was acting in your best interest?
- How can you learn to trust God more during these times?

Prayer: *Loving Father, open my eyes to see You to every situation in my life. Help me to trust that You are always for me, even when my human nature doesn't feel like it.*

Pursue: For a deeper dive, study Romans 8:28–39.

Perceptions: Record any ideas God puts on your heart from this devotion.

RIGHT BESIDE US

Cherokee Indians practiced a strange rite of passage from boyhood to manhood. A father brought his son into the forest, blindfolded him, and left him sitting on a stump. The father commanded the boy to sit there the entire night, without removing the blindfold, until he could detect the rays of the morning sun. He was not allowed to cry out for help but required to sit silently.

Once the boy survived the night, the tribe considered him a man. He could not tell anyone of the experience, because other boys needed to endure this ritual. Throughout the night, with no weapon, the noises of the forest were intense. But he sat unmoving, never touching the blindfold. Finally, after a long restless night, the sun appeared. Removing his blindfold, he instantly discovered something amazing. His father had been sitting on the stump, right beside him all night long!

What an amazing picture of how our Father watches over us. When I face fearful situations, when the noises of anxiety increase in my mind, when I'm blindfolded and stressed about the future, my Father is sitting right beside me. Like the Cherokee lad, I can't see Him, but He's there. Nowhere does the Bible ever promise that

God will prevent us from facing fear. But He promises to be with us in the midst of fear. In Isaiah 43:2 God assures us, "When you pass through the waters, I will be with you; and when you pass through the rivers, they will not sweep over you. When you walk through the fire, you will not be burned." In verse 5 He adds, "Do not be afraid, for I am with you."

Our Father, who knows everything and sees everything, present, and future, wants to make it really, *really* clear that He is *always* with us. Even at three a.m., when our fears place us on a mental torture rack and sleep eludes us. Maybe it's worry over the future because of a job loss. Or the agony of a marriage that's failing and we're powerless to fix it. Or the heart-wrenching sorrow over the death of someone we love dearly. Or sitting on a stump in the middle of the woods all night long. Breathe easy. Our Dad is sitting right beside us, watching over us, protecting us from all harm.

Principle: God is always with us, even when we don't feel His presence.

Promise: "Do not be afraid, for I am with you." (Isaiah 43:5)

Ponder:

- At what times do you most need the assurance that God is always with you?

- When you sense God's presence in a fearful situation, what does this do for you?

Prayer: *Loving Father, thank You for Your promise to never leave me. When I'm afraid, fill my heart with the assurance of Your presence.*

Pursue: For a deeper dive, study Isaiah 43.

Perceptions: Record any ideas God puts on your heart from this devotion.

A BOOK IN A BARREL

In 1833 Abraham Lincoln and his business partner, William Berry, were going broke in their country store. Lincoln told him, "I wouldn't mind so much if we could sell everything we've got and pay all our bills and have just enough left over to buy one good book, *Blackstone's Commentary on English Law*. But I guess that is an impossible hope."

Shortly afterward, a wagon pulled up. "We're plumb broke," the driver said. "Would you be willing to buy a barrel for fifty cents?" Lincoln started to wave them off, but his compassion was stirred when he saw the despair in the eyes of the settler's wife. Handing him his last fifty cents, Abe purchased the barrel. Later, rolling it to a corner of the store, Lincoln heard something moving around. Reaching inside, he pulled out a book... *Blackstone's Commentary on English Law*.

Mere coincidence? I don't think so. Studying Blackstone led Lincoln into a law career, leading him to become a well-known trial attorney, leading him to debate against slavery, leading him to run for public office, leading him to be elected president of the United States, leading him to guide our nation through its greatest crisis, the Civil

War, ultimately saving our republic. All of which began with a book in a barrel. A specific book, in a specific barrel, found by a specific man, at a specific time. God's hand was behind it, leading this great president to save our nation.

Scripture tells us that God is at work in our circumstances as well. "It is God who works in you to will and to act in order to fulfill his good purpose" (Philippians 2:13). Yet the Lord is not some divine puppeteer, manipulating our every move. He chooses to partner with us as He works (1 Corinthians1:9; 2 Corinthians 6:1). The Lord moves in our lives in the same way He presented Lincoln with an opportunity. Seize the opportunity like Abe did!

In all of the uncertainty swirling around us, perhaps we wonder where God is. Take heart; He hasn't forsaken us. He's working right in the midst of the confusion. We don't need to know what He's doing or how He's doing it. In fact, we couldn't understand it, even if He told us. But He's working behind the scenes in our circumstances, and He sees exactly what we need. Just as He did the day when Abraham Lincoln changed the world by finding a book in a barrel.

Principle: God is at work, moving behind the scenes in our lives.

Promise: God works in us to fulfill his purpose

Ponder:

- What specific "book-in-a-barrel" experiences have you faced?
- What opportunities is God presenting you now that you need to pray into and act upon?

Prayer: *Lord, give me wisdom to see where You're working and how I need to respond.*

Pursue: For a deeper dive, study the book of Esther.

Perceptions: Record any ideas God puts on your heart from this devotion.

ATTACK OF THE KILLER VACUUM

Picture a sixty-five-pound English bulldog, hiding under our bed, trembling in terror from a vacuum cleaner. Rosebud was a chunk of pure muscle, equally tall, long, and wide. Her jaws possessed vice-like strength. Although her disposition was as sweet as candy, she was invincible against any foe. Rosebud feared nothing... except our vacuum.

As soon as the vacuum powered on, she raced under our bed to hide from the beast. As the enemy advanced toward her, Rose dashed from her bunker, snarling and biting her metal nemesis. Then retreating briefly, she reemerged a few moments later to resume her foolish assault. Truly, a laugh-out-loud moment. Of course, Rosebud had absolutely nothing to fear from our vacuum. But her simple canine brain convinced her it was a deadly foe. Silly dog!

I wonder how often do I allow my anxiety to overwhelm my faith? Social media, nightly news, and naysayers can drive us scurrying under the bed like a dog running from a "killer vacuum." It's easy for the terrors of the temporal to smother us with unfounded fears—all based on lies. Second Timothy 1:7 states, "God has not given us a spirit of fearfulness, but one of power, love and sound judgment" (HCSB). Consider the implications. Obsessing on my fear is not from God. If God doesn't fill us with fear, then who does? Could it be…Satan?

Of course we'll face fearfulness, but when it rises up in us, it's critical to look to God. Like David. When he faced Goliath, David didn't talk about how dangerous Goliath was. He talked about how great God was. Let's not talk fear. Talk faith.

Rosebud's fears kept her in bondage. Imagine being enslaved to a vacuum cleaner! That (literally) sucks! But it's easy to do. We live in anxiety-ridden times. The world is going crazy, paranoid over everything from politics to pandemics. These may be legitimate concerns, but they can easily weigh us down with worry. Let's look to God for deliverance, not what the world offers. That only creates more anxiety.

 Next time we feel threatened, be it a meeting with our boss, an unpaid bill, or our kid's report card, think of Rosebud and laugh out loud. Remember, God has not given us a spirit of fear, but a spirit of power. He lives in us, and we have nothing—absolutely nothing—to fear.

Principle: When we experience fear, look to God.

Promise: God has not given us a spirit of fear, but a spirit of power.

Ponder:

- What unwarranted, "vacuum-cleaner" fears trouble you?
- When you feel attacked with fearful anxiety, how can you look to God for deliverance?

Prayer: *Almighty God, I praise You, for You possess all power. Remind me of that truth when I feel anxiety rising up within me.*

Pursue: For a deeper dive, study 1 Samuel 17.

Perceptions: Record any ideas God puts on your heart from this devotion.

FIVE QUESTIONS

"There's no such thing as a dumb question." I hate to disagree, but over the years, I've heard (and even asked) a plethora of, let's just call them, "less-than-intelligent interrogative inquires." Here are samples of actual questions asked in court by attorneys:

1. Were you present in court this morning when you were sworn in?
2. Was it you or your brother who was killed in the war?
3. The youngest son, the 20-year-old, how old is he?

Okay, that's enough silliness. In our journey through life, some questions are infinitely more important than others. Especially during these difficult days. If you're like me, sometimes we wake up and immediately feel overwhelmed with anxiety and fear—financially, relationally, vocationally, and every other kind of "ally."

One morning, as I was wrestling in prayer over these worries, the Holy Spirit downloaded five questions that set me free. Immediately, I jumped up, grabbed some paper, and wrote them down. Here they are:

1. Does God *always* want what's best for me? (*Yes*. See Jeremiah 29:11.)
2. Is God powerful enough to come through and take care of *any* problem (*Yes*. See Ephesians 3:20.)
3. What has God promised in His word? (*To provide for me*. See Matthew 6:33.)
4. What's God's track record? (*So far, His track record for getting me out of difficult days is 100 percent*.)
5. Is there any reason to think God won't do it in the future? (*Based on the first four questions, unquestionably no*!)

First Peter 5:7 instructs us to "cast all your anxiety on him because he cares for you" (see also Psalm 55:22). So why not try it? It's so simple…but it's not easy. My mind starts reeling with "what-ifs," immediately upon my eyelids popping open. But I've discovered, in the midst of the wild waters of worry, these five questions keep me afloat. They bring me back to the Rock of Reality, where I'm anchored in truth. God *does* want what's best for me. He *is* powerful enough to solve any problem. Over and over He's *promised* to provide. And He's done so *every* day of my life. So I have *every* reason to believe He will now.

During these turbulent times, rehearse these questions, remind yourself of the answers, and remember (at least with the Lord) these are anything *but* dumb questions.

Principle: In the midst of a difficult day, we need to remind ourselves of the reality of God's care and provision.

Promise: God cares for us and will provide for us.

Ponder:

- Under what circumstances and time of day do you most struggle with anxious thoughts?
- After rehearsing these five questions, how have you found them to be helpful?

Prayer: *Lord God, thank You for your provision through the years, even under difficult circumstances. Help me to continue to trust You in the future.*

Pursue: For a deeper dive, study Psalm 91.

Perceptions: Record any ideas God puts on your heart from this devotion.

THRASHING IN BARBED WIRE

We still don't know how it happened. Linda was home alone when our neighbor frantically knocked on the door. She said a deer was caught in a barbed-wire fence, and her kids were freaking out. Grabbing some wire cutters, the two set out on a heroic journey to free the creature. It ended up being more challenging than they imagined. Approaching the deer, the distraught animal began feverishly kicking and thrashing. This only intensified its entanglement. Even the soothing words of my wife, aptly dubbed "The Animal Whisperer," didn't calm it. Eventually the thrashing subsided long enough for Linda to begin snipping away the wire. Once again, more kicking. Pausing long enough for the poor beast to settle, she resumed her snipping. After repeating this process numerous times, eventually the deer was released. Limping away to a tentative freedom, the deer appeared less than grateful, even though its savior cut and wounded herself in the process.

How often do we find ourselves in a tangled mess, overwhelming our lives with anxiety? Like this unfortunate deer, the harder we try to free ourselves, the more entrapped we become. We're helplessly ensnared.

Eventually, we decide to call out to God, and He shows up to free us. Then the fight is on, as we struggle against his method of liberating us, because it often involves facing unpleasant truths about ourselves and adjusting our behavior. Finally, when we cease thrashing, we let go and trust God. Then He frees us. We can sure act like dumb animals sometimes!

How can we free ourselves from such anxiety? God's only prerequisite is to acknowledge we *need* rescuing. In Luke 18, Jesus told a story about a religious man and a notorious sinner, both praying to God. The religious man waxed eloquently about his wonderful qualities. The sinful man hung his head and cried out, "God, have mercy on me, a sinner" (v. 13). Jesus added, "This man, rather than the other, went home justified before God" (v. 14) Why? He *knew* he needed rescuing. Whether it's the first time we open ourselves up to God, or the thousandth, the process is the same. Want to be free of those anxiety-laden entanglements? Like the deer, you can't do it on your own. Ask God for deliverance, be still, and then *let Him* help you.

Principle: Only God can deliver us from our anxiety-laden entanglements.

Promise: When we acknowledge we need a Savior, Jesus comes to our rescue.

Ponder:

- What specific choices do you make that continue to leave you entangled?
- How do you need to stop "thrashing" and allow God to deliver you?

Prayer: *Blessed Savior, thank You for hearing my cry and rescuing me when I find myself entangled in my own poor choices. Help me to be still and allow You to save me.*

Pursue: For a deeper dive, study Luke 18:9–14.

Perceptions: Record any ideas God puts on your heart from this devotion.

MOTHER MARY COMES TO ME

In 1969 The Beatles were on the verge of dissolving. Only Paul felt motivated to keep the legendary band together. In the midst of deep isolation and rejection, McCartney found comfort in the form of a dream. As he slept, his mother Mary (who had died when McCartney was ten years old), came to him. The essence of her message was: Don't fight it; accept what's happening.

Paul McCartney awoke and wrote the classic hit "Let It Be." Destined to be the last single The Beatles released prior to breaking up, it also claims the honor of the Fab Four's last number-one song in the US. Perhaps you assumed, as did I, that "Mother Mary" referred to the mother of Jesus. Not so. Stirred by his artistic nature, McCartney left the song open to interpretation. In a later interview, he acknowledged that his mum's message was "very reassuring," providing the hope he needed at that moment.

Let...it...be. Three simple words. Not especially profound (unless they're spoken by your dead mother). But their truth is timeless. Some of the best known "refrigerator magnet verses" herald this theme:

- "Be still and know that I am God." (Psalm 46:10)
- "They that wait upon the Lord shall renew their strength." (Isaiah 40:31)
- "Trust in the Lord with all your heart and lean not on your own understanding." (Proverbs 3:5)

In a sense, these spiritual gems could be summed up with that singular phrase, "Let it be."

Whether Paul McCartney's dream was real or imagined, I'll let you decide. But know this. It's not necessary for us to be part of the most famous musical group in history, nor do we need a nocturnal visitation from a dead relative to experience the truth of this principle. These promises from God's Word are always available to provide strength and assurance.

Every day of our lives we face anxious and stressful situations. I'm embarrassed to admit how often I fail to run to Almighty God for strength. But He's always available. Whatever we go through, the Lord continually reassures us with His promises, reminding us, when we find ourselves in times of trouble, turn to God and "Let...it...be."

Principle: When we face anxiety and stress, turn to God and "let it be."

Promise: "They that wait upon the Lord shall renew their strength." (Isaiah 40:31)

Ponder:

- What situations and people d[...]
  entrust to God, and "let it be?"
- What Scriptures and promises fro[...]
  Word offer the most assurance to you?

Prayer: *Lord, when I find myself stressing and worrying, please bring to mind a promise from Your word and help me run to it for strength.*

Pursue: For a deeper dive, study Isaiah 40.

Perceptions: Record any ideas God puts on your heart from this devotion.

SENCE

lion eyeing a baby
...g its chops, the cat advances. Eventually the cub spots the cougar, and the chase is on. Climbing onto a dead limb, the bear plummets into a creek, and drifts ashore where the predator awaits. Death appears imminent. Desperate, the baby stands on its rear legs, extends its tiny paws and issues a high-pitched growl. Incredibly, the mountain lion retreats. Then the camera pans to a wider view, revealing the mama bear, a full-sized grizzly, standing behind her cub.

This nature film mirrors what many are experiencing these days. Anxiety, stress, worry—the what-ifs feel overwhelming. The harshness of our political climate, the threat of natural disasters, and day-to-day family issues bear down on us like a hungry mountain lion. How do we respond? Just like that baby bear. We can't chase off all the wild beasts we encounter. But our Papa can; and He's promised to always be near us, even on those knot-in-our-stomach days. In Hebrews 13:5 God promises, "I will never [under any circumstances] desert you [nor give you up nor leave you without support, nor will I in any degree leave you helpless]" (AMP).

That's convincing! Rely our own resources, and we'll be eaten alive. But remain close to Papa, and we can live fearlessly. God is bigger than any adversity we'll ever encounter, whether real or imagined—bigger than our bills, our bosses, and our burdens. That's why God revealed through Zechariah the prophet as he was facing overwhelming challenges, "Not by might nor by power, but by my Spirit" (Zechariah 4:6). We can live in total reliance on Him, because no adversity is too great for the Lord.

Edwin Friedman in *A Failure of Nerve* shares that our culture desperately needs "a non-anxious presence." Imagine remaining so connected to our Father that our lives are saturated with a non-anxious spirit. Imagine bringing a non-anxious presence into every arena of life: our jobs, families, neighborhoods. I cannot fathom anything more crucial than posturing a non-anxious presence before a fear-filled world. Starting today, let's determine to adopt that mindset. Let's demonstrate what a fearless life looks like. Let's recall the image of that mama bear and remember our "Papa Bear" is always with us.

Principle: We can maintain a non-anxious presence in our world today, because our Papa is always with us.

Promise: God will never desert us, nor leave us helpless.

Ponder:

- In what areas of life do you need to adopt a non-anxious presence?
- In the week ahead, what commitments can you make so this becomes a reality?

Prayer: *Abba Father, turn my eyes toward You. Help me sense Your presence when the "mountain lions" of life attack me.*

Pursue: For a deeper dive, study Psalm 23.

Perceptions: Record any ideas God puts on your heart from this devotion.

IN FEAR'S GRIP

I had just dozed off for a peaceful nap when a bloodcurdling scream jolted me awake. My six-year-old grandson, Jeb, was playing in our backyard and found an exposed wire. Like most curious boys, he grabbed hold, but then discovered he couldn't let go. Hearing Jeb scream, I raced out the back door and shoved him on the chest, knocking him clear. Other than a few blisters on his hand, Jeb was unharmed. But he learned a valuable lesson about respecting electricity. And I learned a valuable lesson about not leaving an exposed wire within the reach of a six-year-old.

Ever grab hold of something and you can't let go? Among other things, fear can paralyze us as quickly as an electrical jolt. Right along with its "close cousins" stress and anxiety, once fear gets us in its grip, it's disabling. Our minds obsess on our worries, as we toss and turn at three a.m. Our psyches reel with a host of unrealistic "what-ifs." But like Jeb, no matter how hard we try, we can't shake it. In fact, the more we attempt to fix our troubles in the middle of the night, the more overwhelming they appear.

Know which command occurs most often in the pages of Scripture? "Fear not." This phrase is found 170 times in the King James Version. God's not a harsh parent placing impossible demands on us. He wouldn't direct us to forsake fear unless it was possible to live free from it. But we can't accomplish this by our own willpower. Only enlisting God's unlimited power can free us.

First Samuel 21 records David fleeing for his life from King Saul. Desperate, David found himself in the land of the Philistines, Israel's greatest enemy. Even worse, in the city of Gath, Goliath's hometown. He didn't exactly receive a hero's welcome, and barely escaped alive. To celebrate his liberation, he penned these words, "I sought the Lord, and he answered me; he delivered me from all my fears" (Psalm 34:4). When we find ourselves in fear's grip, like Jeb we need a push from an outside force. Jesus possesses the power to deliver us from all our fears. Focus on Him, seek Him, and, as David and Jeb did, cry out and He will run to us with the help we need. It's so wonderful, it's shocking!

Principle: Jesus possesses the power to break fear's grip on our lives.

Promise: God will deliver us from all our fears.

Ponder:

- What specific fears tend to wake you up in the middle of the night?

- What steps can you take to turn to God during times of anxiety and stress?

Prayer: *Almighty God, in the midst of fear and anxiety, remind me to look to You and trust in Your power to deliver me.*

Pursue: For a deeper dive, study Psalm 34.

Perceptions: Record any ideas God puts on your heart from this devotion.

HOUSE OF CONFUSION

The sign read, "House of Confusion," located on Highway 42 in Southwest Oregon. Our kids were young, and for a brief instant I wondered if it was describing our home on Friday afternoon. In reality it was an optical illusion attraction, where marbles roll uphill. The house is built so that it appears to defy gravity. Never having visited the spot, the kids and I decided to check it out. Linda waited in the car. The look in her eyes said, "I need some alone time."

I don't remember much, except leaving with a headache. The place certainly lived up to its name. Every room seemed to defy gravity. Short folks appeared tall, and tall folks short. And yes, marbles did roll uphill. Or so it seemed. At one point the guide held a level against the wall, and was I shocked! What appeared to be uphill was actually downhill. I left, having learned a good lesson that day (besides never to take the kids anywhere without Linda). Things are not always as they appear. The eye can be deceived. The level cannot.

In many ways we find ourselves living in a house of confusion today. Uncertainty and uneasiness cloud our brains. Conflicting voices bombard us with information, generating more anxiety and stress than any time in history. The media, Google, our feelings, our friends. Don't you wish you could turn off your mind sometimes? Who's right? Who's wrong? What's real and what's fake news? Just trying to figure it all out sends you to bed with a migraine. We need some sort of spiritual level. Thankfully, the Lord has given us one—the Bible.

The Bible has stood the test of time, proving itself to be a reliable guide for our lives, no matter how things appear in this house of confusion. Psalm 119:105 states, "Your word is a lamp for my feet, a light on my path." Why keep stumbling in the dark when you have a light? I can rest easier knowing there is a spiritual level to show us how to live. Google, our friends, the media—they supply information. But if we need light and truth and *real* answers, look to God's Word. To free our minds from confusion, anxiety, stress, and fear, open the Bible. Ultimately, everything else is just an illusion, like the "House of Confusion."

Principle: God's Word provides the answers we need in these confusing times.

Promise: God's word is a lamp to our feet and a light to our paths.

Ponder:

- How does confusion create anxiety and stress in your life?
- What specific situations cause you to feel the greatest confusion?

Prayer: *God of truth, thank You for Your Word. Help me find comfort in it, when I feel confused and stressed.*

Pursue: For a deeper dive, study these "I Am" statements of Jesus: John 8:12; 10:7; 14:6.

Perceptions: Record any ideas God puts on your heart from this devotion.

AN ORDINARY GOD

How many of us believe in an ordinary God? Researchers in Britain went door-to-door surveying residents about their beliefs in God. They asked, "Do you believe in a God who intervenes in human history, who changes the course of affairs, and who performs miracles?" One man responded, "No, I don't believe in that God; I believe in the ordinary God." His answer so impacted the researchers that they entitled the study "An Ordinary God."

An ordinary God? What does that mean? In reality, God is *anything but* ordinary. In every possible way, He's extraordinary. Ephesians 3:20 states that God "is able to do exceedingly abundantly above all that we ask or think" (NKJV). Let your imagination run wild for a moment, dreaming of everything possible God might accomplish. God is not only able to do more than you can imagine. He's not only able to do abundantly more than that. He's able to do *exceedingly*, abundantly more than we could ever possibly imagine. Paul's choice of words takes on the form of a child's vocabulary: "Humungous, Fantabulous, and Ginormous!"

But it gets even better. In verse 16, Paul prays, "that out of His glorious riches he may strengthen you with power through his Spirit in your inner being." God wants to release His miraculous power into our lives, combining His "super" with our "natural" for a "supernatural" experience. He's waiting for us to ask.

I wonder if I really do believe in "An Ordinary God?" When faced with a crisis, I frequently run right past Him, grasping for my own solutions. I fret and fuss, with blood pressure spiking and headache pounding, forgetting how the extra-ordinary God is on the job, keeping His promise to abundantly supply my needs.

God loves to do extraordinary things through ordinary people. People like me. Every morning I need reminding that whatever I'm facing in the day ahead, God is on the move. I don't need to understand what He's up to, or even like how He does it. I just need to surrender the day to Him. Relying solely on my own resources leads to epic failure, whether it's my health or family or how much I *don't* have in my bank account. In reality, I possess the supernatural power of the Almighty Creator God who lives in me. Not the "ordinary God." He doesn't exist. Because everything...*everything* about Him is extraordinary.

Principle: Everything about God is extraordinary. He can do anything.

Promise: God is able to do exceedingly, abundantly beyond all that I can ask or imagine.

Ponder:

- What challenges are you currently facing that you need to surrender to the Extraordinary God?
- How can you engage deeper in a personal way with God, enabling you to draw on His power?

Prayer: *Almighty God, Fill me with the power of Your infinite presence each morning. Keep me plugged into You as I go through my day.*

Pursue: For a deeper dive, study Isaiah 40 and Psalm 29.

Perceptions: Record any ideas God puts on your heart from this devotion.

KNOCKED OUT BY THE BELL

In 1896 Norman "Kid" McCoy was the reigning world welterweight boxing champion. On one occasion, he was fighting a contender with the misfortune of being deaf. Upon discovering his opponent's disability, McCoy wasted no time in taking advantage of this handicap. Near the end of the third round, McCoy stepped back and pointed to his adversary's corner, indicating the bell had rung. "Oh, thank you so much," said McCoy's opponent. "Very civil of you." However, the round hadn't actually ended, and as soon as the other boxer dropped his hands and turned away, McCoy knocked him out!

While we might admire his ingenuity, in some ways Kid McCoy's tactics represent those of our enemy. The devil operates solely on the basis of lies, half-truths, and deception. When he tempted Eve, Satan began with a question. "Did God *really* say…?" (lying by implication). He followed with a bold-faced lie, "You will *not* certainly die." Then landing his knockout punch, he delivered a half-truth: "You will be like God, knowing good and evil" (Genesis 3:1–5).

In a sense, every struggle we face results from believing some lie of the devil. Am I fearful? I'm believing the lie that God won't take care of me. Do I feel others don't like me? I've swallowed Satan's lie that I need the approval of people. We're in a fight to the death with the enemy (1 Peter 5:8). I can't drop my guard for a moment. Satan's in the ring, hoping to knock me out. Let's make certain we aren't "deaf" to his tactics.

Our current times reflect Satan's operations. Following the devil's lead, our world system spews out lies and deception like a fire hydrant. It's pretty much impossible to know what to believe anymore. "Fake news" is as prevalent as fleas on a mangy dog. Whether it's politicians, network news, or friends on social media, fact-checking is now an essential part of life. Even then, it's not enough to casually check our sources. To be certain, we must dig deep, because often we can't even trust the fact-checking websites.

In the midst of so much uncertainty and anxiety, it's so refreshing to follow Jesus. As God's Son, He is the embodiment of Living Truth. In John 14:6 He declares, "I am the way and the truth and the life." We can believe Him, trust Him and rely on *every* word He says. And *that's* the truth!

Principle: Satan operates on the basis of lies, half-truths, and deception.

Promise: Jesus is the embodiment of Living Truth. We can trust Him.

Ponder:

- How do your current cultural conditions affect your attitude toward truth?
- How can you learn to trust Jesus more?

Prayer: *Lord Jesus I praise You for You are Truth. Increase my faith so that I trust You more.*

Pursue: For a deeper dive, study Psalm 19:7–14.

Perceptions: Record any ideas God puts on your heart from this devotion.

JOY IN THE MOMENT

"Don't be dejected and sad, for the joy
of the LORD is your strength!"
(Nehemiah 8:10 NLT)

"In times of joy, we all wish we
had a tail we could wag."
(W. H. Auden)

LIVING BEER

Imagine returning from a trip, opening your faucet for a cool refreshing drink of water, and a different liquid gushes from the tap. A fellow from New Zealand experienced this firsthand. While on a short trip with his wife, his friends came over, crawled under his house, unhooked the water lines and connected kegs of beer to every spigot. Arriving home, he and his wife turned on the water and were shocked to discover New Zealand ale pouring out. One by one, they repeated this process with every faucet in the house and obtained identical results. Eventually, he stepped outside where his friends were waiting to surprise him. In the end they all shared the brew together.

For beer drinkers, that sounds like a dream come true. But imagine what it would be like to brush your teeth in beer. Or take a shower? Or wash your face? Beer, Kool-Aid, or soda just wouldn't cut it. There's really only one liquid that satisfies our basic need in life: the cool, refreshing, life-giving liquid we long for...water.

Scripture uses the metaphor of "living water" to describe the abundant life we experience in Jesus. In John 7:38

Jesus promised his followers, "rivers of living water will flow from within them." I don't totally understand all the implications, but it has a lot to do with the abundant life Jesus desires for us. Jeremiah 2:13 presents the contrast: "My people...have forsaken me, the spring of living water, and have dug their own cisterns, broken cisterns that cannot hold water." Rather than seeking the abundant life Jesus offers (living water), do we chase after the gods of this world, such as popularity, pleasure, prosperity, or power? As much as our flesh desires them, these are broken cisterns, holding stale water, which cannot fulfill.

For those of us riddled with anxiety, this is really good news. We don't need to exhaust ourselves pursuing the broken cisterns of this world. The living water of Jesus washes over us, saturating our souls with lasting peace.

This world fails to satisfy our deepest thirst. But the living water of Jesus fulfills us. Which brings us back to our beer story. As much as the Kiwis enjoyed it, when the beer ran out, they didn't dash to the store for more kegs. They hooked up their water once again. Because whether it's real or metaphorical, what we long for, what we really need, is cool refreshing water.

Principle: Only the living water of Jesus fulfills us.

Promise: The living water of Jesus saturates our souls with peace.

Ponder:

- When do you most sense my need for the living water of Jesus?
- What anxious thoughts do you need to surrender to Jesus and allow Him to saturate with living water?

Prayer: *Jesus, I release every anxious thought to You. Saturate me with Your water of life.*

Pursue: For a deeper dive, study John 4:1–15 and 7:37–39.

Perceptions: Record any ideas God puts on your heart from this devotion.

SLEEPING IN THE ENTRY

Doug and Sylvia White had high hopes as they opened the door to the bridal suite of an expensive hotel late at night. The room contained a sofa, two chairs, and a table...but no bed. They discovered the sofa was a hide-a-bed, with a lumpy mattress and sagging springs. The honeymooners settled for it but slept fitfully and awoke with sore backs.

The next morning, the groom went down to the front desk and verbally let loose on the manager. The clerk tried to speak, but the husband was on a roll. Finally, he took a breath, and the manager jumped in. "Did you open the door to the room?" Doug went back. He opened the door they had assumed was a closet. There was the honeymoon suite, complete with king-sized bed, Jacuzzi, and champagne. Rather than enjoying the luxurious room they paid for, they spent their wedding night in the entryway to the honeymoon suite.

How often do we settle for sleeping in the entry when Jesus wants us to experience the honeymoon suite? God has given us His "very great and precious promises" (2 Peter 1:4), which include freedom, hope, and joy. Rather than grasping hold of these promises and living in the victory of Jesus, perhaps we plop down on a spiritual sofa bed and sleep in the entry. God hasn't called us to merely hang on and survive; he wants us to thrive. We weren't delivered just to settle for the entryway, but to enjoy the honeymoon suite. Even in our struggles, he wants us to live out of a place of victory. Romans 8:37 tells us that "overwhelming victory is ours through Christ."

Does this passage characterize our lives? Our struggles attempt to steal our victory in Christ. At times I vacillate between the honeymoon suite and the sofa bed. I allow anxiety and stress to creep in, and before I know it, I've grabbed my blankie and I'm tossing and turning on a hide-a-bed. I've left my overwhelming sense of victory sleeping soundly in the bridal suite. Let's not allow anxiety to steal our triumph. Remember the promises God has given us and live in a place of victory. Open the door to the honeymoon suite and experience God's blessings. Jesus is waiting for you!

Principle: God wants us to live in a place of victory.

Promise: God has given us His very great and precious promises.

Ponder:

- What anxious thoughts drag you out of the "honeymoon suite" and into the "entryway"?

- What promises from God could you meditate on to fill you with a sense of victory?

Prayer: *Jesus, You died so I could live in victory. Bring me back to that place where we share Your victory together.*

Pursue: For a deeper dive, study Romans 8.

Perceptions: Record any ideas God puts on your heart from this devotion.

PEA-SIZED PROBLEMS

My daughter, Tiffany, was entering first grade and required an inoculation. When we shared this tragic news with her, Tiff immediately went into panic mode. It didn't exactly sound like a trip to Disneyland to get violently stabbed in the arm with a giant needle (at least that's the story her six-year-old mind was visualizing). She fretted over it all evening. Tucking her in, I assured her she had nothing to fear, and we prayed...but it didn't help. The next morning, I repeated my encouragement, with the same futile results. Driving her to the doctor, I could practically taste the fretful fear in our vehicle.

No sooner had we entered the doctor's office than a child's scream erupted from the back room. Turning to each other, we made eye contact, and I read my daughter's mind: "That's gonna be me in a few minutes." Eventually, we were called back. After seating Tiffany, a kind nurse dabbed a swab of alcohol on her arm. Tiff managed to moan out her final request. "Please tell me when you're about to give me the shot."

Smiling, the nurse looked at Tiffany and said, "Honey, I just gave you the shot." Tiffany hadn't even felt it! All the anxiety; all the stress; all the fretting was for nothing! A look of relief washed over Tiff's face, and a huge grin broke out. She had endured a twenty-four-hour mental torture rack of her own making…for nothing!

Aren't we all guilty? We turn a pea-sized problem into a stadium-sized fear. Perhaps Franklin Roosevelt had this in mind when he uttered his famous declaration, "We have nothing to fear, but fear itself." It's why Jesus repeatedly instructs us, "Do not worry" (Matthew 6:25–34). It's why he often asked His disciples, "You of little faith…why did you doubt?" (Matthew14:31). It's why more than 170 times God tells us to "fear not." Because fearful fretting is our default.

Like Tiffany, we make our paranoia bigger than our problems, our trepidation larger than our troubles. The next time we face some frightful situation, let's dismiss that voice in our heads. Before we let our minds run wild, let's pause and put the situation in perspective. Take those thoughts captive and surrender them to Jesus. He promises to calm our fears (John 14:27). We'll quickly discover what we think are stadium-sized problems, don't amount to a hill of peas!

Principle: Our problems are almost never as big as our fears.

Promise: Jesus will calm our fears.

Ponder:

- What pea-sized problems do you tend to turn into stadium-sized fears?
- How can you reverse this tendency and trust God with your anxious thoughts?

Prayer: *Lord Jesus, in the midst of my anxious thoughts, You tell me to "fear not." Remind me of my human tendency to make my fears bigger than my problems.*

Pursue: For a deeper dive, study John 14:1–27.

Perceptions: Record any ideas God puts on your heart from this devotion.

THE WINNING TEAM

The spray from the can discharged, blasting me in the face, followed by more bursts of fizz. My son's pee-wee football team had won the championship. As their coach, these fifth-grade boys were showering me with soda, just as the pros drench their coach with champagne. I willingly endured this ritual, because as sticky as the process was, nothing compares to being part of the winning team.

Each year, the two best teams in the NFL square off in the Super Bowl. Billions of dollars are poured into the pigskin panorama. Millions of cheers and tears arise across the land, as a new champion is crowned. A hero's welcome awaits the victors. Nothing compares to being part of the winning team.

The book of Revelation presents a powerful picture of the ultimate winning team. If we view this volume as a crystal ball, it's easy to miss its victorious message: "Jesus won." Even in the midst of His people's brutal persecution on earth, Christ proclaims His victory through His resurrection. "I died, but look—I am alive forever and ever! And I hold the keys of death and the grave" (Revelation 1:18). When Jesus rose from the dead, He crushed the power of Satan, securing eternal victory.

Despite appearances, we know the end of the story—we know who won. The Bible's last chapter reveals the final score. In Revelation 22:5 God assures Team Jesus, "They will reign forever and ever." Here on earth, it's easy for fear and anxiety to grab us in its grip. But remember, we've already won through Jesus. Right now, we're in the fourth quarter waiting for the clock to run out. Satan is still trying to take a few of us out of the game. But don't despair. Let's hold our heads high and live in a place of victory.

Revelation 2:10 promises, "Be faithful, even to the point of death, and I will give you life as your victor's crown." Every player on the winning Super Bowl team receives a victor's ring. It matters not if you're the MVP or a benchwarmer. Because of Christ's victory, our Super Bowl ring awaits us. As we're weighed down with fear, as we face agonizing adversity, remember the outcome is already decided. Above all remember, nothing compares to being part of the winning team.

Principle: Nothing compares to being part of the winning team.

Promise: "Be faithful, even to the point of death, and I will give you life as your victor's crown." (Revelation 2:10)

Ponder:

- When you truly believe you're on the winning team, how does this change your life?
- In what specific areas in life do you need to engage Jesus as the All-Powerful Conqueror of death?

Prayer: *Thank You for the victory I have in You, Jesus. In the midst of struggle, remind me that I'm on the winning team forever, and lift my head above my outward circumstances.*

Pursue: For a deeper dive, study Revelation 21 and 22.

Perception: Record any ideas God puts on your heart from this devotion.

THE ROLLING ROOFTOP

During his lifetime, my brother-in-law Roger owned a house-moving company. He would crawl under a house, jack it up, lower it onto huge dollies, hitch a truck up to the house, and drive it down the street, like it was a VW. A couple of times when we visited him in Seattle, he asked me to help on a moving job. I'm far from being famous for my agility, so my guess is, he must've really been desperate for help. On one occasion, he assigned me the task of standing on the rooftop and lifting up traffic lights as the house rolled down the road. I figured, "How hard can that be?"

It turned out to be about as challenging as scaling the Eiffel Tower…blindfolded. Imagine straddling the apex of a house as it moved down the road, maneuvering a 100-pound traffic light in the air, all the while maintaining my balance so as not to tumble to an untimely death. Then pivoting as the house moved past the intersection, slowly returning the light to its original position. All in all, a life-or-death challenging experience.

Sometimes life's like that, isn't it? Ever have one of "those days;" or maybe a series of "those days"? Like my ordeal on the rolling rooftop, everything seems to come at us at once. The car won't start, the toilet backs up, the principal from the kid's school calls. Demands come at us from every side: work, family, friends, church. On those days, it's easy to feel overwhelmed. We cry, "It's too much!" Is it possible, rather than allowing ourselves to feel overwhelmed, to trust God with everything life throws our way, without letting it deliver a knockout punch?

During his lifetime, Jesus experienced many "rolling rooftop" days. Mark 6:31 states Jesus and His apostles were so busy "coming and going that they did not even have a chance to eat." But Jesus never let it phase Him. (Remember how He fell asleep in the middle of a storm?) That's because He knew how to rest in the Father's presence...which is exactly what we need to do. This isn't rocket science, but putting it into practice is about as easy as threading a needle in the dark. However, resting in His presence changes everything. A supernatural peace engulfs us, enabling us to handle whatever comes our way. Especially on those "rolling rooftop" days.

Principle: We all experience "rolling rooftop" days.

Promise: Resting in God's presence fills us with supernatural peace.

Ponder:

- How does the picture of Jesus resting in the storm inspire you to trust God more?
- In what specific areas of your life do you need to practice trusting God more?

Prayer: *Lord, on those "rolling rooftop" days, fill me with Your presence and give me a heart of peace.*

Pursue: For a deeper dive, study Mark 3:13–5:20. (This is one day in the life of Jesus.)

Perceptions: Record any ideas God puts on your heart from this devotion.

THE BEST WAY TO KILL ZOMBIES

It began with a simple question. My two teenage grandsons were in my back seat on the way home from school. They raised a question of profound significance. "What's the best way to kill zombies?" A debate ensued between them. A chainsaw? A bat with nails? An AR-15? They locked onto their opinions like a zombie on meat, and it was game on. The debate quickly escalated into a verbal Gettysburg. At this point I interrupted the conflict, reminding them that zombies are fictional, hence to knock off the fruitless discussion. I might as well have been mumbling in my sleep.

By the time we arrived at their house, I feared they were on the verge of fisticuffs. Ever the concerned grandpa, I pulled up, ordering them to get out. Listening to their conversation, one would conclude the entire future of the cosmos hung on discovering an answer to this dilemma. I drove away shaking my head at the utter foolishness of worrying over something that has a zero percent chance of happening.

Then I wondered, how often do I allow my anxieties to exaggerate a concern that has no basis of truth? I begin obsessing over finances or work or kids. Before you can say "living dead," I'm stressed-out over a fear so far removed from reality, you can't even recognize it. Much like my grandsons, I'm all worked up over a bizarre fantasy.

According to a University of Michigan study, 98 percent of our worries never happen. Pause and think about that. We create ulcers, make ourselves miserable, and strain our relationships over stuff that's not going to happen. Once we step onto "Anxiety Avenue," it's hard to reverse our tracks.

Philippians 4:6 tells us, "Don't worry about anything; instead, pray about everything" (NLT). Even while being pursued by a maniac who wanted him dead, David wrote, "There's no risk of failure with God. So why would I let worry paralyze me?" (Psalm 62:2 TPT). To make sure we get it, he repeats this in verse six. Reflect on those statements. They sure sound a whole lot better than tossing and turning at night, fretting about stuff I can't change. Whether we're going in for a job interview, a meeting with our kid's principal, or being chased by zombies, anxiety is a waste of time, health, and life. There really is no risk of failure with God!

Principle: Worry about nothing; pray about everything.

Promise: There's no risk of failure with God.

Ponder:

- What zombie-like fictional fears are you nursing?
- How does the promise that "there's no risk of failure with God" offer you assurance?

Prayer: *Lord, You are in charge of all things. There's no basis for any fear. Free me from the "zombie worries" I create in my mind.*

Pursue: For a deeper dive, study Matthew 6:25–34.

Perceptions: Record any ideas God puts on your heart from this devotion.

EYES ON THE MASTER

Chloe, our Boston Terrier, doesn't always mind so well. I can't seem to break her of the annoying habit of jumping on company, as her tongue flicks at light speed in an effort to "kiss" them. Surprisingly though, I've succeeded in training her to obey a much more difficult command.

Directing Chloe to "sit," I place a piece of meat on the floor in front of her and order her to "wait." She remains as still as a stone until I state, "Okay." Then she gobbles it as voraciously as a vulture on a carcass. It's perplexing. She can't restrain herself from jumping on strangers but finds the strength to resist a delicious morsel of meat.

Then I noticed something. As Chloe sits facing the meat, she doesn't look at it. Instead, she fixes her eyes on me, her master, until I give her the word to eat.

When we face tests in any form, whether temptation, adversity, or fear, how often do we focus on our struggles, rather than our Master Jesus? While on earth, Jesus came to His disciples on a lake, walking on the water. One of the disciples, Peter, stepped out of the boat and miraculously began walking toward Him. As long as

Peter kept his eyes on his Master, he could operate in the supernatural. But the moment he looked at his struggles (the wind and waves), his heart filled with fear and he sank like concrete (Matthew 14:30).

The lesson is obvious. Keep our eyes on the Master and not on our messes. Psalm 123:2 states, "As the eyes of servants look to the hand of their master, as the eyes of a female slave to the hand of her mistress, so our eyes look to the Lord our God." When we adopt this practice of focusing on the Master, God promises we will "fear no evil" (Psalm 23:4).

Viewing all the uncertainty in our world, like Peter, we can begin to feel overwhelmed with fear. But continuing to bring our focus back onto our Master fills us with peace. The journey is so much sweeter. And when Satan dangles his meat in front of us, we won't be pulled away, because, like Chloe, all we can see is the face of our Master.

Principle: Focusing on our Master, rather than our fears, frees us to experience supernatural peace.

Promise: When we remain focused on the Master, we will fear no evil.

Ponder:

- What fears or struggles are you focusing on in your mind?
- How can you turn your eyes upon Jesus in the midst of difficulties?

Prayer: *Lord Jesus, You give me strength in the midst of my fears. When I become distracted by the concerns of this world, turn my eyes toward You.*

Pursue: For a deeper dive, study Matthew 14:22–33.

Perception: Record any ideas God puts on your heart from this devotional.

THE FOG OF FEAR

Driving in fog is not only dangerous but it also can be downright deadly. A blanket of vapor can force traffic to a standstill, grind business to a halt, and even shut down airlines. The National Bureau of Standards reports that a dense fog covering seven city blocks to a depth of 100 feet is comprised of approximately 60 billion tiny droplets. Yet if all those droplets were brought together, they would fill less than one glass of water. But that one cup of water possesses the power to cripple a city.

I wonder how often I empower "60 billion water droplets" to fog my thoughts and steal my peace? Especially when it amounts to nothing more than a cup of water! Certainly, major tsunamis come crashing into our lives at times: divorce, cancer, addiction...but those are entirely different "weather systems." I'm referring to the simple day-to-day concerns we grossly enlarge, which can ravage our psyches like a horde of Huns.

The fog of fear obscures our vision and distorts our perspective. When we find a barrage of tiny droplets fogging us in ask, "How much does this *really* matter?" Will I even remember this a month from now (or even in a day)? We fuss and fret over a host of teeny troubles that only amount to a cup of water!

How do we deal with the fog of fear when it creeps into our lives? By looking to Jesus. Driving through fog, the sun still shines above the fog line. Likewise, in the throes of a spiritual fog, we can be confident that the Son shines on us as well. In Psalm 94:19 King David wrote, "Whenever my busy thoughts were out of control, the soothing comfort of your presence calmed me down and overwhelmed me with delight" (TPT). When those tiny droplets of fear fall on our hearts, pause and take a deep breath. As you exhale say, "Lord, I give everything and everybody to You." The fog in your heart will slowly evaporate as Jesus, the Light of the World, burns through the gloom (John 8:12). Let's not allow the fog of fear to block the Son-shine from our lives.

Principle: Jesus, the Light of the World, can clear the "fog of fear" from our hearts.

Promise: "Whenever my busy thoughts were out of control, the soothing comfort of your presence calmed me down and overwhelmed me with delight." (Psalm 94:19)

Ponder:

- What "tiny water droplets" are stealing the joy in your life?

- When you feel "fogged in," how can you allow the "Son-shine" to burn brightly once again?

Prayer *Lord, You see all things clearly. Reveal to me those worries and concerns that are "fogging" my life. Please flood my heart with Your light and burn away the fog.*

Pursue: For a deeper dive study Psalm 94.

Perceptions: Record any ideas God puts on your heart from this devotion.

IS GOD DEAD?

Shortly after his marriage to Katharina von Bora, the great reformer Martin Luther was experiencing extreme persecution, which led him into bouts of depression. Arriving home one day, he found his wife dressed in black, wearing a mourner's veil. Luther froze. "Who died?'

"God did," she replied.

Stunned, Luther asked, "What do you mean? Of course God didn't die! How can you say such a thing?"

She stopped, stared at him, and replied, "Based on how you're acting, I can only assume that God must be dead." Some tough lady!

Depression can wreak havoc in even the hardiest of hearts. Sure, some folks suffer from clinical depression, caused by chemical imbalance. But I'm confident the majority of our depression, anxiety, and worry results simply from thinking the wrong thoughts. We center our minds on our misery, rather than our Messiah. We forget who our Father is, that He's in charge of the universe and loves us more than we can imagine. God is not dead!

David experienced his share of depression, and in the throes of despair penned these words in Psalm 13:1–2, "How long, Lord? Will you forget me forever? How long will you hide your face from me? How long must I wrestle with my thoughts and day after day have sorrow in my heart?" (Let me paraphrase: "God, are you dead?")

In verse four, David turns his eyes to the Lord in prayer. Notice the transformation in tone that follows: "But I trust in your unfailing love; my heart rejoices in your salvation. I will sing the Lord's praise, for he has been good to me" (vv. 5–6).

David's mood swing wasn't the result of anti-depressants. It came from anti-depressing thoughts! And the same is true for us. We're living in times that could suck the joy out of Mr. Rogers. Just facing the day-to-day issues arising from family, friends, and finances can feel overwhelming. But now we're dealing with the pandemic, and all the fallout it dumps into our lives. We're stuck at home. We're tired. We're lonely. We're battling depression—much like Martin Luther…and David. So what's the answer? Katharina von Bora nailed it. Turn our thoughts away from our troubles and onto our triumph. Remind ourselves of all we can be grateful for. Pause in His presence. Our circumstances may not change. But we can remember…God is not dead!

Principle: In the midst of our struggles, remember that God is alive.

Promise: My Father is in charge of the universe and loves me more than I can imagine.

Ponder:

- On a scale of one to ten, how prone are you to depression?
- What thoughts and Scriptures can you meditate on to help during difficult times?

Prayer: *I praise You, Lord. I trust in Your unfailing love. My heart rejoices in Your salvation.*

Pursue: For a deeper dive, study Psalm 13.

Perceptions: Record any ideas God puts on your heart from this devotion.

EYE OF THE STORM

In June 1957 category-four Hurricane Audrey blasted the Gulf Coast of Louisiana. The torrent claimed 416 lives, the deadliest hurricane from 1938 until 2005. Being only four years old at the time, I possess sketchy memories of the storm. However, I recall praying for our neighbor's horse, which I feared might perish in the deluge. My father later shared that in the middle of the night, he and my mother suddenly awakened and bolted upright in bed, gasping. Not as a result of the noise, but because of the deathly silence. We were in the eye of the storm, and for the next hour it remained eerily quiet, before resuming.

We often employ storms as metaphors for struggles. Experiencing adversity, we say we're passing through "rough waters" or "stormy seas." We might refer to peaceful times as "smooth sailing." We expend much effort attempting to avoid the storms of life, but such endeavors are futile. In John 16:33 Jesus promised, "In this world you will have trouble." Expect storms. On occasion we face hurricanes—those rare tragedies such as divorce, cancer, or the death of a loved one. More often, we experience the constant whirling of the winds of anxiety.

At times, life got a little crazy for Jesus as well. On one occasion, He and His disciples were so busy that they didn't even have a chance to eat (Mark 6:31). But He stayed calm. Even in a "furious squall" on the Sea of Galilee, as the apostles were certain of imminent death, Jesus fell asleep on the boat (Mark 4:35–41). He was able to rest in the midst of a terrifying storm, because He lived in the *eye of the storm*, where all is surrendered to God.

Life is filled with storms; we can't avoid them. But we can rest in them. Just like Jesus. The second half of John 16:33 reads, "But take heart! I have overcome the world." Thank God, in the midst of our anxious, stressed-out times, we have that promise. As the wind and waves of life rage around us, we can surrender our storms to the Creator of the storms, because He faced them and overcame them all. We can simply close our eyes and rest, knowing it's in His hands. Then surrender the storm again, as often as needed, and begin to live in peace in the eye of the storm.

Principle: There is peace in the eye of the storm, knowing Jesus is with me.

Promise: "Take heart! I have overcome the world." (John 16:33)

Ponder:

- What specific storms are you currently facing?
- How can you pause and rest with Jesus in the eye of those storms?

Prayer: *Lord Jesus, thank You for showing me how to face my storms. I praise You that You have overcome the world. Give me strength to face my storms each day.*

Pursue: For a deeper dive, study Mark 4:35–41.

Perceptions: Record any ideas God puts on your heart from this devotion.

OTHER DOGS' BUSINESS

I only need to utter one simple word: "Walk," and Chloe, our Boston Terrier, is bouncing for joy at the front door. With her adjustable leash connected, we head down our road. Chloe is off and running in every direction. She zigs and zags from one side of our lane to the other. Nose to the ground, Chloe sniffs out every dog in the neighborhood. She's constantly on the alert for a cat or chicken to chase...and the queen mother of all doggie delights: a disgusting substance to wallow in. What's amazing about Chloe's walks is the amount of energy she expends. For every mile I walk, Chloe covers four. By the time we return home, she plops down in her doggie bed, exhausted.

Know what actually wears Chloe out? Not our walk. It's sticking her nose in all the other dogs' business. She worries so much about what all the other neighborhood creatures are up to, she's exhausted when we return.

We share a lot in common with our furry friends. On our journeys through life, what wears us out aren't the tasks God assigns to us. He always supplies the strength we need for each moment. What exhausts us is trying to mind other peoples' business. Think of all our worries and concerns. Don't they usually involve other people? We fret over what others think of us, or the choices our kids make, or what kind of mood our boss might be in. We create so much anxiety for ourselves by minding other peoples' business.

And if we're not worried about other peoples' business, we're fretting over God's business. As if we need to make certain that the Great I AM is or isn't performing in ways we think He should! God reminds us, "Stay calm; mind your own business; do your own job" (1 Thessalonians 4:11 MSG). How much stress, worry, and anxiety would we save ourselves if we practiced these simple instructions? We each have enough individual struggles to manage without minding other peoples' business.

Philippians 4:7 promises that when we surrender our concerns and those of others to God, we experience "the peace of God, which transcends all understanding." When we find ourselves worrying over what others are doing, pause. Give it to God. We'll find our lives are much less stressful when we stop minding other peoples' business.

Principle: Our lives are less stressful when we cease worrying over other peoples' business.

Promise: Surrendering the concerns of others to God, we experience peace that transcends understanding.

Ponder:

- In what specific ways would your life be less stressful if you learned to stay calm, mind your own business, and do your own job?
- What steps can you take to make this a habit?

Prayer: *Lord Jesus, make me aware when I'm trying to mind other people's business, and help me to center my thoughts on You.*

Pursue: For a deeper dive, study 2 Thessalonians 3:11–15.

Perceptions: Record any ideas God puts on your heart from this devotion.

MOVING A-HEAD

In 2015 an Italian doctor claimed he could perform a human head transplant within two years. Dr. Sergio Canavero, a neuroscientist from Turin told leading doctors that he had begun initial preparations and even had a volunteer. Two years later, he alleged to have made good on his claim, boasting he had successfully "realized the first human head transplant." That sounds amazing—until we add one tiny detail…it was performed on a corpse! That last piece of information changes things, doesn't it?

The scientific community isn't exactly racing to embrace Dr. Canavero. Skeptical doesn't begin to describe their attitude. Besides medical hurdles, huge ethical concerns must be overcome. Many doubt the good doctor's motives. But if you ask me, he's just trying to stay "ahead" of the competition!

Reading this, my mind flashed to images of Mel Brooks' *Young Frankenstein*. Sure, we've made huge advancements in medicine, but jumping over the moon might be easier to achieve than a head transplant. Biblically, understanding that we each possess a unique spirit created in God's image, presents insurmountable obstacles.

But in a sense, Scripture teaches that when we say yes to Jesus, God gives us a "head transplant." He renews our minds. It's a process, but a reality nonetheless. Ephesians 4:23 tells us that in becoming more like Jesus, there must be a spiritual renewal of our thoughts and attitudes (or a "head transplant"). Romans 12:2 instructs us to "let God transform you into a new person by changing the way you think" (NLT).

During these times, it's critical we embrace this truth. So many are freaking out over what's going on in our world. It's time for brain surgery. Our old thought patterns of anxiety and fear need to be cut off and transplanted with a new brain dominated by faith and courage. Despair and hopelessness must be removed and replaced with our new minds of hope and peace. Anger makes way for compassion. And on and on. Our Father is the Master Surgeon, and He never makes mistakes. As good patients, our part is focusing on things that are "true...noble...right...pure...lovely" (Philippians 4:8). We can start by not obsessing on the news.

Head transplants are nothing new. God successfully performs them every day. And be assured He always operates out of love for us. As for Dr. Canavero, he needs 15 million dollars to accomplish this medical breakthrough. Anyone care to donate?

Principle: Our times call for a change in our thoughts and attitudes

Promise: Let God transform you into a new person by changing the way you think.

Ponder:

- What old ways of thinking do you wish to be free from and to replace with a new mindset?
- What attitudes and behaviors do you need to let go of and to partner with God in His surgery?

Prayer: *Lord, You are the Master Surgeon. Open my mind to receive Your life-changing surgery.*

Pursue: For a deeper dive, study Ephesians 4:17–32.

Perceptions: Record any ideas God puts on your heart from this devotion.

CONNECTED TO JESUS

In 2009 police arrested a Florida man for ramming his car into a church building. Claiming that he wanted to be "closer to Jesus," officers discovered Phillip Wagner's car partially inside Faith United Methodist Church. Damage to the church was estimated at about $10,000, and Wagner was placed in the county jail under suicide watch.

Aside from Mr. Wagner's emotional instability, at least we can admire his desire to be closer to Jesus. His unorthodox actions speak to our common human longing for a deep union with our Creator. Thankfully, no one needs to ram a car into a church building to be closer to God. In John 14:23, Jesus promised His followers, "My Father will love you so deeply that we will come to you and make you our dwelling place" (TPT). Jesus lives in us. We can't get any closer to Him than we already are!

In John 15:5, Jesus used a different metaphor to describe His union with us: "I am the vine; you are the branches. If you remain in me and I in you, you will bear much fruit; apart from me you can do nothing." It's not necessary for a branch to grunt and groan in order to bear fruit. Only one thing matters: staying connected to the vine. The vine draws energy from the sun and nutrients from the soil and...guess what? Fruit happens! But cut it off from the vine, and it dies.

Never has this been truer than during these unstable times, when anxious thoughts whirl through our minds like a vortex. At the risk of sounding overly-simplistic, Jesus said if we stay connected to Him as we move through our days, we will experience real life. We will discover incredible peace in the midst of anxiety. Wonderful release from worry. Freedom from fear. Simply by remaining connected to Jesus. There's no other way to achieve it. Self-effort and human solutions can offer temporary relief. But none can deliver what Jesus can long-term.

A tool that helps me stay focused on Jesus is the Pause app by John Eldridge. Download it to your phone and give it a try. It requires effort to focus on Jesus in the midst of all the distractions and anxieties of life. But it's sure worth it. Besides, it's a whole lot easier (and less expensive) than ramming your car into a church building.

Principle: Remain connected to Jesus and experience real life.

Promise: As followers of Jesus, we can be assured that He lives in us.

Ponder:

- How does remaining connected to Jesus free you from anxiety?
- What steps can you take to stay connected to Jesus each day?

Prayer: *Lord Jesus, I invite You into my heart. Fill me with Your presence.*

Pursue: For a deeper dive, study John 15:1–17.

Perceptions: Record any ideas God puts on your heart from this devotion.

FRET NOT

Steve Tran of Westminster, California, left his small apartment one morning and closed the door behind him. Prior to leaving, he activated twenty-five bug bombs, attempting to rid his apartment of cockroaches. But when the spray reached his stove's pilot light, it ignited, blasting his screen door across the street, breaking all his windows, and setting his furniture ablaze. He later commented, "I really wanted to kill all of them. I thought if I used a lot more, it would last longer." As it turns out, two canisters were all he needed. The blast caused over $10,000 in damages to his apartment. And as for the cockroaches, Tran reported, "By Sunday, I saw them walking around."

There's nothing cuddly about cockroaches. But I wonder what would drive a man to set off enough bug bombs to destroy an apartment? Then again, we all possess our own variety of cockroaches that "bug" us—those anxieties and phobias we wrestle with. At times they can change, depending on how our day goes. We're late to a meeting. Our kid's principal calls—not with good news. We forget to record a debit in our checkbook…and, well, you get the picture.

Then there are those cockroaches which constantly plague us. Concern over an adult child haunted by addiction. Struggling to make ends meet. Constant anxiety over what others think of us. We all find ourselves wishing we could set off enough bug bombs to blow them out of existence.

Psalm 37 records David's struggle with some of his cockroaches; specifically, why do the wicked seem to prosper? The psalm begins with a two-word command, "Fret not," which is repeated twice more in the chapter. He permeates the psalm with these injunctions: "trust in the Lord...delight in the Lord...be still before the Lord...hope in the Lord." Anyone notice a thread of thought? Every day of our lives, we'll be plagued by cockroaches in some form. They come and go, but as David declares, the Lord is the one constant who endures.

We don't need twenty-five bug bombs to rid ourselves of our pesky anxieties. When our cockroaches return, as they did with Steve Tran, focus on the Lord, not our anxieties. It matters not if it's an IRS audit, a visit from our mother-in-law, or even cockroaches, God's instruction is the same: "Fret not!"

Principle: Every day of our lives we face anxieties ("cockroaches") in some form.

Promise: The Lord is our one constant who endures, not our anxieties.

Ponder:

- What anxieties plague you most in your life?
- How can you focus on the Lord when they return?

Prayer: *Lord, thank You that You are the one constant I can rely on when I am plagued by my anxieties. Help me not to fret but to rely on you.*

Pursue: For a deeper dive, study Psalm 37.

Perceptions: Record any ideas God puts on your heart from this devotion.

HOPE & REALITY

"Hold on to the hope that is ours. This hope is like an anchor for us. It is strong and sure and keeps us safe."
(Hebrews 6:18–19 ERV)

"Hope is being able to see that there is light despite all the darkness."
(Desmond Tutu)

MY GARDEN OF HOPE

"How could this happen?" Slumped on a bench, I buried my face in my hands. Our garden's gurgling fountain and blossoming fruit trees sharply contrasted my gloom. The bank was foreclosing on our home, where we had lived for seventeen years. Our children grew up in this house. Sequestered in our garden, I cried out to God. Due to our poor investments, a sense of failure enveloped me like a wool blanket. "Lord, forgive me. We've lost it all. What will we do now?"

As I sat there, God reminded me of His promises. I recalled Matthew 6:33, "But seek first his kingdom and his righteousness, and all these things will be given to you." He brought Philippians 4:19 to mind: "God will meet all your needs according to the riches of his glory in Christ Jesus."

Suddenly, these realities hit me. God didn't need our money or our house. He could provide in ways we could never imagine. If losing our home meant we needed to depend more on Him, then so be it. I paused, as a sensation of freedom touched my heart. My Father owns everything—I own nothing! I was trusting in material possessions more than Jesus. In that moment, God released a profound peace over me.

From that moment everything was different, even though outward circumstances remained unchanged. The bank repossessed our home, and we relocated. Certainly, we experienced periods of deep sorrow. But looking back ten years to that moment on my garden bench, I'm overwhelmed by God's sovereign ways of provision and the hidden blessings He birthed from this heartbreak.

He opened a door for us to buy a country home on two acres with our daughter's family, significantly lowering our housing costs. Today, we experience the joy of living next door to our grandchildren. God gives us opportunities to minister to others who have lost their homes. None of this would have occurred had we remained in our dwelling. Ultimately, God provided for us far better than we ever imagined.

Jesus promised to meet our needs. Just as Israel constructed stone monuments to remember God's great deeds (see Joshua 4:20), my garden experience serves as a spiritual marker, reminding me that God never fails us. No matter how external circumstances appear, He always comes through, transforming a garden of despair into a garden of hope.

Principle: God has unlimited resources and will provide for us in surprising ways.

Promise: God will meet all your needs according to the riches of his glory in Christ Jesus.

Ponder:

- When have you experienced God's unexpected supernatural provision?
- What situations do you need to surrender to God and trust Him to provide?

Prayer: *Lord, thank You for the promise to supply our needs. Strengthen me to trust You, even when I don't see any possibilities.*

Pursue: For a deeper dive, study Philippians 4:10–20.

Perceptions: Record any ideas God puts on your heart from this devotion.

TOO EARLY TO TELL

An old man and his son lived together in a small village. One night their stallion broke down the corral and escaped. His neighbors came and said, "Oh that's bad." He wisely replied, "Maybe it is; maybe it isn't. It's too early to tell." The next morning the stallion returned, leading three mares. This time the townsfolk said, "Oh that's good." Again the old man replied, "It's too early to tell."

The following day his son fell off one of the mares and broke his leg. Ever ready to offer their opinions, the villagers cried, "Oh, that's bad." The old man stuck to his mantra: "It's too early to tell." After that, the king sent his soldiers and enlisted all the young men to fight in a war...except the old man's son who broke his leg. Care to guess what the villagers said and how the old man replied?

"It's too early to tell." We all should have that phrase inscribed across our lives. Don't assume simply because something looks bad, it's the end of the story. Scripture overflows with examples of those who had every reason to believe "that's bad," only to discover "it's too early to tell."

Think of David. He was anointed as future king of Israel. (That's good.) Then King Saul tried to kill him. (That's bad.) But David escaped. (That's good.) Then he hid in a cave from Saul. (That's bad.) Eventually, he took possession of the throne. (That's good.) Each of these points were snapshots in David's life. None represents the full picture.

In the midst of this stressful ping-pong match, David settled his anxious heart with this assurance of God: "You are my prize, my pleasure, and my portion. I leave my destiny *and its timing* in your hands" (Psalm 16:5 TPT).

Whatever you're experiencing at this moment, don't assume it's settled. Who knows how God might take what we define as bad and use it for good? Is there the slightest possibility that God just might have a broader picture of our future than we do? We all know the answer to that question. Next time your back is against the wall and you find yourself muttering, "That's bad," pause for a moment. Remember this story. Thank God He's working in our lives. Put your trust in Him, because "It's too early to tell."

Principle: Before we decide the outcome of a situation, remember "It's too early to tell."

Promise: "I leave my destiny and its timing in your hands." (Psalm 16:5 TPT)

Ponder:

- What situations are you in the midst of, in which you've already assumed a negative outcome?
- When have you encountered a similar situation that turned out well?

Prayer: *God, I praise You for seeing the end before the beginning. I place my life's circumstances in Your hands, especially those where it's too early for me to tell the outcome.*

Pursue: For a deeper dive, study Psalm 18 and 34.

Perceptions: Record any ideas God puts on your heart from this devotion.

SANDCASTLES

I stood on the beach, my toes pressing in the sand. Before me lay Windsor Castle, the Eiffel Tower, and Golden Gate Bridge, all entries in a sandcastle contest at a local beach. With mouth gaping, I marveled at the detail of these structures, even snapping some pics. Then as I walked away, it hit me. These sandcastles were made of sand (duh!). When the tide came in, they would all be swept way, no matter how beautiful.

Jesus used this metaphor in Matthew 7:24–27: "Anyone who listens to my teaching and follows it is wise, like a person who builds a house on solid rock. Though the rain comes in torrents and the floodwaters rise and the winds beat against that house, it won't collapse because it is built on bedrock. But anyone who hears my teaching and doesn't obey it is foolish, like a person who builds a house on sand. When the rains and floods come and the winds beat against that house, it will collapse with a mighty crash" (NLT).

Without Jesus, no matter how lovely, powerful, or prosperous our lives may appear, when the storms hit or the tide comes in, we'll be washed out to sea like those sandcastles. That's true of us all.

We've all met folks whose lives are like a sandcastle in a storm. Externally, they abound with superficial beauty. But like those sandcastles, there's no solid foundation. Look at our world right now. Whatever we've trusted in for security appears to be crumbling in the tide of trouble. A pandemic shuts down the world. Huge economic and emotional losses follow, after weeks of quarantine. Bankruptcies, domestic violence, and suicides are skyrocketing. Out-of-control violence rages in cities across our land. If we wonder what's going on, look at what Jesus taught. Build our lives on anything other than Him, and we'll be washed out to sea.

The world promotes fear and hopelessness. Jesus, our Rock, offers life, hope, freedom, and truth. He calls us to stand on the rock and live radically different lives from the world around us. To bring heaven to earth (Matthew 6:10), reflecting the love and light of Jesus to a confused world. To rise above the lies and darkness of this world. To let go of the false security our culture offers. Because anything other than Jesus is simply a beautiful sandcastle.

Principle: What our world offers is like a sandcastle in a storm.

Promise: Build our lives on Jesus, and we're on a rock.

Ponder:

- What are the "sandcastles" in your life that you tend to trust in for security?
- What steps can you take each day to deepen your foundation on the Rock?

Prayer: *Jesus, I thank You that in this world of sinking sand, I can run to You for security. When I forget, remind me that You are my Rock.*

Pursue: For a deeper dive, study Psalm 62.

Perceptions: Record any ideas God puts on your heart from this devotion.

A DANGEROUS FOX TROT

Bystanders must have shaken their heads in wonder at a woman running down a path with a live fox dangling from her arm by its teeth. Near Prescott, Arizona, a lady was jogging when a rabid fox attacked her. The creature bit her on the foot, so she grabbed it by the neck. Then the situation worsened. The rabid animal latched onto her arm. The woman wanted it tested for rabies, so she ran a mile to her car with the fox still hanging on her arm. She pried it off, tossed it in her trunk, and drove to the Prescott hospital.

As serious as this is, I can't help smiling when I imagine this scene. But it's not so humorous when we encounter "rabid foxes" in our lives. Anger over the current conditions of our world, fear of the future, and frustration over being powerless to do anything about it. These negative mindsets can be just as dangerous as running through life with a rabid fox dangling from your arm. Clamping their jaws on us, it's nearly impossible to pry these foxes off.

Song of Solomon 2:15 pictures our life as a vineyard with foxes wreaking havoc as they run through it: "Catch for us the foxes, the little foxes that ruin the vineyards, our vineyards that are in bloom."

The answer is not to fixate on the foxes, but to rise above the troubles of this world and live in God's peace. Colossians 3:1–3 reminds us, "Yearn for all that is above, for that's where Christ sits enthroned at the place of all power, honor, and authority...fill your thoughts with heavenly realities, and not with the distractions of the natural realm...your true life is hidden away in God in Christ" (TPT).

That's not easy to do. The foxes of this world constantly snap at us, through the media and those around us. They attempt to pull us down from a heavenly mindset and distract us with the concerns of the natural realm. When that happens, we need to pause in His presence and turn our thoughts toward heaven. Remember that's where our real life is. Whether it's politics, pandemics or the pursuit of pleasure, these distractions are minimal when cast in the light of eternity. Let's lift our eyes above to our true life, turn away from the distractions that pull us down, and don't get caught up in a dangerous fox trot.

Principle: The distractions of this world pull us down from living in God's peace.

Promise: Your true life is hidden away in God in Christ.

Ponder:

- What "foxes" (distractions) attach themselves to you and pull you down?
- How can you rise above them?

Prayer: *Lord, You promise that my true life is in You. Lift my mind above the distractions of this world and center my thoughts on heaven.*

Pursue: For a deeper dive, study Colossians chapter three.

Perceptions: Record any ideas God puts on your heart from this devotion.

CAN I HANDLE YOUR BAGGAGE?

The sights, the sounds, and the smells of India greeted me as I stepped out of our taxi at the Chennai train station. Talk about a chaotic sensory overload! Thousands of people milled about like ants. A cacophony of noise arose, as confusing as the Wall Street Stock Exchange. I smelled a mix of human sweat, garbage, and smoke. It was like nothing I'd ever experienced...and I was enthralled by it all. Once we were stationary, a horde of porters barraged our party, desperately desiring to handle our baggage. Our host, Babu, negotiated with them, and quicker than you can say "chicken masala," porters snatched up our bags and toted them off on their heads.

My American "git 'er done" attitude kicked in, and I informed Babu that I was perfectly capable of handling my own baggage. At that moment, I learned an important lesson from Babu. Everyone has a specific role in India. This was the porters' job, so I needed to allow them to do it.

How often do we resist permitting others to handle our baggage? Especially Jesus. In Matthew 11:28–30,

He offers, "Come to me, all you who are weary and burdened, and I will give you rest. Take my yoke upon you and learn from me, for I am gentle and humble in heart, and you will find rest for your souls."

The Message is even more emphatic: "Are you tired? Worn out? Burned out on religion? Come to me. Get away with me and you'll recover your life. I'll show you how to take a real rest. Walk with me and work with me—watch how I do it. Learn the unforced rhythms of grace. I won't lay anything heavy or ill-fitting on you. Keep company with me and you'll learn to live freely and lightly." Here's the "Barney Translation" of that text: "Can I handle your baggage?"

The all-powerful Son of God *wants* to handle our baggage! Why limp through life dragging our baggage when He's asking to take it? Perhaps it's the baggage of religious duty or of uncontrolled anger. Maybe lust, people-pleasing, or entitlement...whatever it is, He's got it! Why be burdened with the baggage of life when Jesus can handle it? Let's guard our egos from kicking in and saying, "I don't need any help." Let Jesus handle our baggage!

Principle: Jesus wants to handle our baggage.

Promise: "Come to me, all you who are weary and burdened, and I will give you rest." (Matthew 11:28)

Ponder:

- What burdens are you most resistant to allow Jesus to carry?
- Where does this resistance come from?

Prayer: *Jesus, I come to You in humility. Forgive me for my pride in wanting to take care of my own needs, rather than rely on You.*

Pursue: For a deeper dive, study Matthew 11:28–30.

Perception: Record any ideas God puts on your heart from this devotion.

STRANGLING THE BEAST

While rock climbing in the high desert, Ray Rathmun tripped and landed face-to-face with a four-foot-long rattlesnake. The instant he moved, the rattler struck, barely missing Rathmun's ear. Its poisonous fangs caught in the threads of Ray's turtleneck sweater. A life-or-death battle ensued. Rathmun began choking the snake, feeling its venom trickling down his neck. The animal squirmed, coiling around Ray's head. Rathmun freed himself from the coils, but again lost his footing and tumbled downward, hauling the snake with him.

Rathmun's predicament worsened. When he fell, his arms pinned on the rocks. Ray still held a tight grip on the snake, but the rattler was within striking distance. Eight times the viper lunged at Rathmun's face. Each time, he turned his face downward so the snake struck just below his eye, fangs unable to penetrate flesh. The battle ended when Rathmun strangled the snake to death, discovering he was unable to let go. He was forced to pry his own fingers loose.

There is a battle you and I wage every day with a different kind of wild animal...the Bible calls it "the flesh." The apostle Paul describes this struggle in Romans 7:15. "I want to do what is right, but I don't do it. Instead, I do what I hate." Then in verse eighteen he adds, "I want to do what is right, but I can't" (NLT).

Sound familiar? It's easy to believe I'm the only one who battles like this with my flesh. But if the great apostle Paul experienced this spiritual tug-o-war between flesh and spirit, suppose I just might as well?

Although we battle in many arenas, one of the greatest beasts we struggle with is anxiety. Simply viewing the evening news can destroy our peace of mind. Sometimes anxiety just comes upon us. But yielding to it can take us out like a deadly viper.

On our own, we're hopeless victims in this battle. Paul declares, "Oh, what a miserable person I am! Who will free me from this life that is dominated by sin?" (v. 24 NLT). He then answers his own question. "Thank God! The answer is in Jesus Christ our Lord" (v. 25). Look to Jesus. Confess our weakness and ask Him for strength. Lean into Him and his victory at the cross. I don't have to strangle the beast by my own strength.

Principle: Our battle with anxiety can be a deadly struggle.

Promise: Jesus Christ delivers us from a life dominated by sin.

Ponder:

- How does reading of Paul's battle with sin offer you hope in your own battles?
- When do you find your battle with anxiety expressing itself in the strongest way?

Prayer: *Lord Jesus, thank You that You have freed me from this life dominated by sin. Give me strength in my battle with anxiety.*

Pursue: For a deeper dive, study Romans 7:14–25.

Perceptions: Record any ideas God puts on your heart from this devotion.

TRAPPED IN A CLOSET

Awakened when his bed caught fire, Edward Sweeney of New York City ran to the door, opened it, and slammed it behind him...only to discover he was in a clothes closet and couldn't get out! Meanwhile, other tenants smelled smoke and sounded the alarm. Firemen came and not only extinguished the blaze but also released Mr. Sweeney from the closet when they heard him pounding on the door.

At times we've all found ourselves trapped in a closet, not knowing how to escape from the blazing inferno. The fire may take the form of a failed marriage, a job loss, a debilitating illness, or the death of a loved one. Talk about anxiety! Our world is up in flames, and we feel helpless and terrified.

As we tremble in this closet we may wonder, "Will I be stuck in here forever? Will this fire consume me?" Our anxious thoughts can eat us alive. Know this—our God sees right through every closet door we find ourselves in. Not only aware, but like a fireman answering a call, He's moving to free us.

Hebrews 2:18 tells us that Jesus went through every struggle we'll ever face, and He stands ready to help us: "Since he himself has gone through suffering and testing, he is able to help us when we are being tested." Jesus understands the anxiety and fear of being trapped in a closet, because He's been there.

Yet in the midst of our anxiety, rather than turn to Jesus, we might run to the arms of a lover, a bottle, or perhaps to the mall for retail therapy. While they can provide a temporary outlet from anxiety, how well do they work long-term? They actually compound our anxiety. When we leave the mall or wake up the next morning, and our problems are there waiting to pounce on us. Only now our guilt engulfs like an inferno. Human solutions don't remove our anxiety. We're still trapped in a closet.

When the room is on fire, run to Jesus. He understands how we feel. Call out to Him, and trust Him to open the door. Fall into his arms, and experience His peace. Real peace. Not the shallow, fleeting promises the world offers. But deep, enduring peace only Jesus can bring. It sure beats staying trapped in a closet in the middle of a fire!

Principle: In the midst of a spiritual or emotional fire, run to Jesus.

Promise: Jesus is able to help us when we are being tested.

Ponder:

- What fire are you currently experiencing or have recently experienced?
- How does knowing that Jesus understands your struggles help you in this?

Prayer: *Merciful Jesus, thank You for understanding how I feel. Thank You for helping me in my time of need.*

Pursue: For a deeper dive, study Hebrews 4:14–5:10.

Perceptions: Record any ideas God puts on your heart from this devotion.

FIVE YEARS OF WATERING

A species of Chinese bamboo possesses a remarkable growth cycle. The owner plants a seed, then waters and fertilizes it for a year with no results. He repeats this process a second year. Still nothing happens. The third year passes, then the fourth. Meanwhile, the farmer continues to faithfully water and fertilize his bamboo seed, witnessing no growth. The fifth year arrives, and something amazing happens. In a period of six weeks, the Chinese bamboo tree grows roughly ninety feet!

Five years waiting for a plant to sprout? Really? But we've all found ourselves anxiously wringing our hands at times, wondering if our situations are ever going to change. Perhaps it's a difficult marriage or a dead-end job or a child who perpetually seems to make poor choices. We feel as if we're endlessly stuck at year four-and-a-half. During those times, God's simple instruction is to trust Him and wait.

In Psalm 40:1 David says, "I waited and waited and waited some more" (TPT). (Can I get a witness?) The word *wait* in Hebrew doesn't mean sitting idly in boredom, staring zombie-like into space. It can be translated "tie together by twisting" or "to entwine." Psalm 27:14 declares, "Don't give up; don't be impatient; be entwined as one with the Lord" (TPT). Waiting provides us with wonderful opportunities to align our hearts with God's purpose, to entwine ourselves with Him. Persevering without tangible results is about as easy as sitting on a hot stove. One minute feels like forever! But it's the means God uses to teach us endurance and trust.

Think of Joseph in the book of Genesis. This young man was sold by his brothers to slave traders. For thirteen years he "sheltered in place" as a slave and prisoner. But the Lord was preparing him for greatness. In one day, the Pharaoh elevated him from a prisoner in a dungeon to ruler of Egypt. I'm guessing Joseph endured many lonely nights—times he may have felt like giving up on God. But he didn't.

When we find ourselves in those seasons of watering and fertilizing, we must not lose hope. Instead, wait upon the Lord. Spend our days becoming entwined as one with Him. Then one day, like Joseph, we'll experience breakthrough and discover our "bamboo" has sprouted ninety feet.

Principle: Do not lose hope in times of waiting on the Lord.

Promise: Entwine our hearts as one with the Lord, and He will carry us through adversity.

Ponder:

- What difficult times of waiting are you currently experiencing or have recently experienced?
- What does entwining yourself with God look like for you on a daily basis?

Prayer: *Father God, help me to entwine myself with You during difficult times. Show me what waiting truly means.*

Pursue: For a deeper dive, study Psalm 25 and 27.

Perceptions: Record any ideas God puts on your heart from this devotion.

GET READY TO BE SURPRISED

A man in Taiwan fell madly in love with a young female. Every day for two years he wrote her a letter proposing marriage, totaling more than seven hundred love letters. Eventually, she fell in love and said yes to a marriage proposal. His efforts paid off...but not for him. She married the mailman who delivered the letters. Surprise!

Life has a way of throwing us unexpected surprises, some less than pleasant. The result is our anxiety levels can rise like rockets. So it's crucial in life to learn to expect the unexpected. Suppose Noah was expecting to build an ark to escape a worldwide flood? Or how about Saul of Tarsus being surprised by Jesus on the road to Damascus? Or Moses being commanded by a talking bush to return to Egypt where he was number one on the most-wanted list? Prepare to be surprised.

In the midst of an anxiety-laden series of surprises, King David wrote, "I would have despaired unless I had believed that I would see the goodness of the Lord in the land of the living (Psalm 27:13 NASB1995). In verse 14 he concludes, "Wait for the Lord; Be strong and let your heart take courage." God supplies courage for those anxious moments, because He is the Lord of surprises. Without that hope, despair would certainly overwhelm us.

Let's get real. Some of life's surprises can leave us twisted in agony. But our Father is in the middle of those anxious moments that accompany every surprise. In fact, our worst surprises often emerge as our greatest blessings. In the end, God used Noah's family to restart the human race. Saul's name was change to Paul, and he became a great apostle. And Moses delivered the Israelites from bondage. God loves to surprise us by turning our burdens into blessings.

Ultimately, did our Taiwanese Romeo find another love upon which to shower his romantic advances? We don't know. But we can be certain of this: life is filled with surprises—some of which taste as bitter as a green lemon. Whenever we face a crisis, we have a choice. Ring our hands in fretful anxiety, trying to fix our situation. Or trust God to turn our unexpected surprises into unexpected blessings. In the end, that's the best surprise of all.

Principle: God loves to turn our unexpected surprises into unexpected blessings.

Promise: "I will see the goodness of the Lord in the land of the living…wait for the Lord." (Psalm 27:13–14 NASB1995)

Ponder

- When has the Lord surprised you by switching a burden into a blessing?
- What other stories from God's Word come to mind that illustrate this truth?

Prayer: *Father, when an unexpected surprise fills me with anxiety, grant me the faith to surrender it to You. I praise You for working behind the scenes, preparing wonderful blessings for me.*

Pursue: For a deeper dive, study Psalm 27.

Perception: Record any ideas God puts on your heart from this devotion.

STANDING

If you asked Robert Samuel what he did today, he might reply, "I just stood around." Because that's what he does. Every day. In fact, that's how he earns his living: just standing around. Robert Samuel is a professional "stander." It's a simple job. He hires himself out to stand in line for other people, earning up to $1,000 per week.

At first that might seem like the most boring job on the planet. Just imagine waiting in line at the Department of Motor Vehicles all day! But by multitasking he could get lots of stuff done: phone calls, paying bills, catching up on his reading...maybe it wouldn't be so bad after all.

In some ways, as followers of Jesus we're commissioned as professional "standers." Ephesians 6:13–14 tells us to, "Put on the full armor of God, so that when the day of evil comes, you may be able to stand your ground, and after you have done everything, to stand. Stand firm..." That's our job description: to stand firm. We stand on the forgiveness Jesus brings at the cross. We stand on the power of Jesus in the resurrection. We stand on the authority Jesus has given us in His ascension. Jesus has already defeated Satan at the cross (Colossians 2:15).

We can confidently "stand" in our victory through Jesus, because we've already won!

Standing doesn't translate into idly twiddling our thumbs in fidgeting monotony. Immediately following his admonition to stand, five times Paul tells us to pray (Ephesians 6:18–20). We pray, and we pray, and we trust in God's power. It's not always as easy as it sounds. It's a continuous dance of surrendering to Jesus as He leads us.

Yes, in that process, the Enemy bombards our hearts with fear and shame. But those anxious thoughts can bounce off us like foam bullets. We boldly stand in our connection with Christ, knowing He's already won. We rest in His peace that is "more wonderful than the human mind can understand" (Philippians 4:7 TLB). That doesn't sound so bad, does it? Let's take our stand on Jesus. Let's rest in Him. And like Robert Samuel, let's embrace our calling as professional "standers."

Principle: I can confidently stand in the victory Jesus won at the cross.

Promise: "When bad times come, you will be able to stand strongly. You will not fall." (Ephesians 6:13 EEB)

Ponder:

- What are some of the fears that Satan bombards your heart with?
- How can you "stand my ground" when he attacks?

Prayer: *Lord Jesus, thank You for Your victory at the cross. I take my stand on You. Remind me of Your victory when times of fear overtake me."*

Pursue: For a deeper dive, study Ephesians 6:10–20.

Perceptions: Record any ideas God puts on your heart from this devotion.

FLYING FIRST CLASS

I glanced at my jet-lagged wife and said yes. On the final leg of a mission trip, I stepped up to the gate as the agent announced, "First class seats are on sale...only $50." One glance at Linda told me this would be the best hundred bucks I ever spent.

Ahh...flying first class. Extra legroom, wider seats, and meticulous service. Economy can't compare. Once when I flew coach, I squeezed into a middle seat next to a woman who fell asleep after takeoff. Slowly her head drifted over until she was leaning on my shoulder. When she awoke, she apologized profusely. Only then did I notice a circle of drool on my shoulder. Linda was amused by the incident, since she was seated next to me by the window.

But flying first class? That's a different story. I didn't miss any of the discomfort of economy. Not for even a moment did I wish we were back in coach, potentially being drooled upon. My heart didn't pine for the narrow seats and cramped leg-room. In first class, we wallowed in luxury.

When we think of heaven, perhaps we worry about missing aspects of life on earth. My kids once verbalized a fear that heaven would be boring. Really? There's nothing about earth we'll miss in heaven, any more than missing coach while flying first-class. All the features of economy are found in first-class...only so much finer! Everything we love on earth will be magnified a million-times over in heaven, with additional surprises God has in store for us!

Think of the greatest joy you've ever experienced on earth. Our most miserable moment in heaven will be infinitely better. Likewise, the ugliest place in heaven will be millions of times more beautiful than earth's most scenic spot. C. S. Lewis referred to earth as "Shadowlands," a mere shadow of blessings to come.

Life on earth holds many joys. But it simply cannot compare to what we'll experience in Paradise. Romans 8:18 promises," Our present sufferings are not worth comparing with the glory that will be revealed to us." Whatever troubles we're experiencing, we can fill our hearts with hope. In heaven, we'll be flying first class... and you'll never need to wipe drool off your shoulder.

Principle: Whatever troubles we experience; we can fill our hearts with hope.

Promise: Our present troubles are not worth comparing with the glory of heaven.

Ponder:

- What aspects of heaven do you believe will be similar to life on earth?
- How will it be radically different?

Prayer: *Lord, fill my heart with a vision for the glories that lie ahead for Your children.*

Pursue: For a deeper dive, study Revelation 21 and 22.

Perceptions: Record any ideas God puts on your heart from this devotion.

LIVING IN A TOXIC WORLD

Off the coast of Mexico lie underwater caves containing deadly levels of hydrogen sulfide, so toxic it kills most organisms within minutes. Yet one creature not only survives in this lethal environment but also thrives—the small Atlantic molly. This tiny fish is a mystery to scientists. Besides living in the midst of poison, this creature actually changes its environment, detoxifying and removing the hydrogen sulfide around it.

In some ways, this furnishes us with a picture of our lives as followers of Jesus. While we experience so many beautiful aspects of life this side of heaven, Scripture is clear that we live in a toxic world. First John 5:19 states, "We know that we are children of God, and the whole world is under the control of the evil one." Ever since the curse fell upon the human race following Adam and Eve's sin, this is the reality of our existence. Personally, I'm not shocked by the presence of evil in our world. I'm pleasantly surprised at how much good there is.

God's call on our lives is not just to survive in our pernicious habitat but to thrive—to transform our environment rather than allowing it to influence us.

Phillips' translation of Romans 12:2 reads, "Don't let the world around you squeeze you into its own mold." Like the Atlantic molly, which transforms its culture, our role is to change our world.

But dont fear; we're not alone. Jesus told the disciples that they would be hated by the world (John 15:18–25). Then in the next verse, He promised to give the Holy Spirit. The presence of God dwells in us, supernaturally empowering us to navigate through our toxic surroundings.

The toxic attitudes of our world—anxiety, stress, fear, negativity—run rampant in our times. These destructive mindsets can poison our thoughts faster than The Flash on steroids. Rising above the toxicity of our culture and soaring to a higher level is a battle we face each day. We have a choice. We can allow the world to drag us down, or we can open ourselves to the Holy Spirit and all the resources God supplies, rising above the fear and negativity the world feeds us. It's a battle, but we can thrive as we live in a toxic world.

Principle: God calls us to thrive in our toxic world.

Promise: God gives us the Holy Spirit, empowering us to rise above the toxicity around us.

Ponder:

- What toxic attitudes do you allow to pull you down, such as anxiety, fear, and negativity?

- How does knowing we live in a toxic world help you face the challenge of anxiety?

Prayer: *Lord, I confess my struggle with allowing the world to influence me. Empower me to rise above it and change my environment.*

Pursue: For a deeper dive, study John 15:18–16:15.

Perceptions: Record any ideas God puts on your heart from this devotion.

A SELF-IMPOSED PRISON

The day after police in England questioned a man about the assault of an 86-year-old woman, he disappeared. Law enforcement never gave up their search for him, periodically popping into his home. Eight years later, they caught him. Incredibly, he'd been hiding in a six-by-two-foot hole under the floorboards of his living room. He concealed himself so well, even his children didn't know he was there. For the first two years of his self-imposed imprisonment he never saw the light of day. Then he began coming out occasionally, and that's when the cops nabbed him.

Imagine enduring eight years in such a miserable existence! Crammed in a dank, dark hole, unable to hug your children or feel the sun on your face. So much more miserable than being locked behind bars! Why not simply surrender in the beginning and do your time?

Yet I wonder, how many of us live in prisons of our own making? Pursuing a path of self-indulgence, selfish-ambition or self-pity, we dig holes for ourselves, existing in self-imposed bondage. Anxiety, worry, and fear are certainly on the short list of those choices that enslave us and keep us locked away from the life God designed for us. He created us for freedom (Galatians 5:1).

Jesus's time-worn promise in John 8:32 rings true. "You will know the truth, and the truth will set you free." In verse 36 he adds, "If the Son sets you free, you will be free indeed." Years ago, I visited a young man in jail who was facing life in prison. He shared, "In jail, I found a freedom I've never known. I'm actually more free now—in jail—than I was on the outside...because now I have Jesus."

In contrast, I talk with people every day who exist in a prison of misery. I don't mean they're behind bars at the "County Hotel." But their self-imposed prison is just as real—and the worst prisons are those of our own making. We can be locked up in a mansion on a hill or in a posh corner office of a high-rise. It's a comfortable prison, to be sure, but it's still a prison. It's odd, because the cell's not even locked! We can walk out anytime, because Jesus has liberated us. We simply need to open the door, accept the freedom He offers, and walk out into a wonderful new life.

Principle: Anxiety and worry sentence us to a self-imposed prison.

Promise: If the Son sets you free, you will be free indeed.

Ponder:

- How might anxiety and worry enslave you in a prison of your own making?
- How can you release them to Jesus and allow him to set you free?

Prayer: *Lord Jesus, I believe You can free me from every form of bondage. Help me embrace Your truth and experience the freedom You promise.*

Pursue: For a deeper dive, study John 8:31–47.

Perceptions: Record any ideas God puts on your heart from this devotion.

GRATITUDE

"In every situation [no matter what the circumstances]
be thankful *and* continually give thanks *to God*; for
this is the will of God for you in Christ Jesus."
(1 Thessalonians 5:18 AMP)

"Often people ask how I manage to be happy despite
having no arms and no legs. The quick answer is that
I have a choice. I can be angry
about not having limbs, or I can be thankful
I have a purpose. I choose gratitude."
(Nick Vujicic)

FORGETTING MONA LISA

"You don't know what you've got till it's gone." We've heard that time-worn cliché a thousand times because it's true. In 1911 the Mona Lisa disappeared for two years. It was stolen. What followed was one of those head-shaking-try-and-figure-this-out experiences. During the two years of its absence, more people visited the spot where Da Vinci's masterpiece had previously rested than actually viewed the Mona Lisa in the two years prior to its theft! Why? Because we don't know what we've got till it's gone. Our human default is to move through life more concerned about what we *don't* have than to focus on the gifts we possess.

God instructs us to relish life's simple blessings. Ecclesiastes 2:24 states, "There is nothing better than to enjoy food and drink and to find satisfaction in work. Then I realized that these pleasures are from the hand of God" (NLT). Rather than wallowing in self-pity over what we're missing out on, let's be thankful for what we have. If we're dining on a hamburger, savor it. Don't sit around wishing we were feasting on steak. We'll make ourselves and everyone around us miserable.

During our quarantine on the *Grand Princess* cruise ship, my family faced this struggle. As we floated on the Pacific, many of our fellow passengers made the most of our extended voyage. Others chose to tread water in the "Sea of Entitlement," constantly complaining about their circumstances. They were angry at the cruise line, angry at the government, angry at the catering company, angry at...I think you get the picture.

While we had our miserable moments, God enabled our family to be grateful for His blessings in the midst of our mess. We soaked in God's presence each morning. Linda guided our grandchildren in creating "gratitude pictures," drawings depicting our blessings. Although it was an effort, we attempted to live in the moment.

When we focus on God's blessings, we step into heaven on earth. But when we forget Mona Lisa (what we have), we remain stuck in a sort of living hell. Thomas Monson reminds us, "Happiness comes when we stop complaining about the troubles we have, and offer thanks for all the troubles we don't have."[2] Life's too short to waste on "if only." As we move through life, let's reflect on what we have, rather than what we don't have. Let's relish each moment, celebrating "Mona Lisa," rather than waiting until she's gone.

Principle: Our human nature is that "we don't know what we've got till it's gone."

---

[2]   Thomas Monson, Inc., January 24, 2020.

Promise: Appreciating our simple blessings creates joy in our lives.

Ponder:

- What simple blessings in your life do you fail to appreciate?
- How can you develop a more grateful heart?

Prayer: *Lord, create in me a grateful heart. Help me to value life's simple blessings.*

Pursue: For a deeper dive, study Ecclesiastes 3.

Perception: Record any ideas God puts on your heart from this devotion.

REMEMBER NOT TO FORGET

Dr. Oliver Sacks, in *The Man Who Mistook His Wife for a Hat*, tells the story of Jimmie G., who suffered from Korsakoff syndrome caused by alcohol abuse. Jimmie G. had experienced total short-term memory loss. Although forty-nine years old, he was convinced he was only nineteen. A battery of tests confirmed his condition. He was shown three objects, which were then covered up. Asked to identify them one minute later, he had no recollection that the objects were ever revealed to him. When put in front of a mirror, he became agitated and confused, believing he was only nineteen. One minute later, he had forgotten the entire incident had occurred.

Such an existence would be like living in an Alfred Hitchcock horror film. However, at times we all suffer from Spiritual Korsakoff Syndrome. In the midst of daily struggles, we often fail to recall the magnitude of God's blessings. But in contrast, gratitude transports us to a different dimension—into the presence of God. Psalm 100:4 states, "You can pass through his open gates with the password of praise. Come right into his presence with thanksgiving" (TPT).

Near the end of his life, Moses warned Israel to "remember not to forget" all God had done for them. He reminded a new generation that when they're settled and satisfied in the Promised Land, to "be careful that you do not forget the Lord" (Deuteronomy 8:11). "You may say to yourself, 'My power and the strength of my hands have produced this wealth for me.' But remember the Lord your God, for it is he who gives you the ability to produce wealth" (vv. 17–18).

We tend to remember God in the wilderness—standing in the unemployment line, sitting in a marriage counselor's office, or waiting in ICU for a loved one to die. But in the promised land, in the midst of prosperity? It's easy to develop memory loss.

Years ago, an episode of *The Simpsons*, portrayed Bart saying grace before a meal. (You can already sense trouble, can't you?). He prayed, "Dear God, we paid for all this stuff ourselves so thanks for nothing!"[3] Gratitude is the cure for a multitude of emotional ills, not the least of which is entitlement and a victim mindset. Korsakoff syndrome can take many forms. "Remember not to forget" is a great mantra to carry us through the most anxious of times.

Principle: It is crucial that we "remember not to forget" God's blessings.

---

[3] *The Simpsons,* "Two Cars in Every Garage and Three Eyes on Every Fish" (1990).

Promise: Gratitude transports us into a different dimension—into God's presence.

Ponder:

- In what specific situations do you most suffer with "Spiritual Korsakoff Syndrome."
- What steps can you take to remember God's blessings?

Prayer: *Lord God, You are so good to us. Thank You for Your blessings. Give us grateful hearts at all times.*

Pursue: For a deeper dive, study Deuteronomy 8.

Perception: Record any ideas God puts on your heart from this devotion.

COMPAIN, COMPLAIN, COMPLAIN

A man joined a monastery where monks were allowed to only speak two words per year. After the first year, the novice met with the abbot who asked, "What are your two words for this year?" He replied, "Food's cold." A year later, when asked to share his two words, he replied, "Bed's hard." Following his third year, he spoke these two words: "I quit!" His superior replied, "Well, I'm not surprised! All you've done since you got here is complain, complain, complain!"

We all can be like this monk at times. In the midst of a really bad day, our complaint meter quickly spikes, and we spew negativity over everyone we encounter, faster than a gossip columnist with a hot story.

God takes a grim view of constant complaining. Concerning Israel in the wilderness, Paul wrote, "Don't grumble as some of them did, and then were destroyed by the angel of death" (1 Corinthians 10:10 NLT). Sounds pretty serious. Know why? Complaining beats others down and equally harms the one dishing out the complaints.

We all prefer the flip side of complaining, which is encouragement. Building others up. Forty-six times the New Testament uses the word *encourage* in some form. As quickly as we flee from complainers, we are drawn to those who encourage us. First Thessalonians 5:11 states, "Encourage one another and build each other up." Like fuel in our tanks, it gives us power to keep going when we're ready to call it quits.

Of course, we encounter stuff we don't like in life. But that's reality. Some situations we can change; others we need to accept. We have a choice. We can accept what is (reality) or we can fight against it, spewing out complaints like a vending machine on steroids, which only increases our stress and that of everyone around us. None of us can change reality. "It is what it is."

Our world furnishes us with lots of fuel for complaining. These times drip with anxiety and fear. But whining and complaining only feeds our anxiety. Rather than giving in to constant complaining, let's run in the opposite direction. Let's speak words of encouragement to others. Let's use our words to dispel seeds of fear and anxiety. And if we ever find ourselves in a place where we can only speak two words a year, let's make sure they're encouraging words!

Principle: Complaining in the midst of our anxious times increases our stress.

Promise: Encourage others and build them up.

Ponder:

- What areas of your life do you tend to complain most about?
- How can you switch your thinking away from complaining to encouraging?

Prayer: *Lord Jesus, You bless us and encourage us with Your presence continually. Please show me how to be more encouraging to others.*

Pursue: For a deeper dive, study 1 Thessalonians 5.

Perceptions: Record any ideas God puts on your heart from this devotion.

LOVINGLY KICKED AROUND

The front feet and head emerge first. Shortly thereafter the newborn is hurled to earth. Falling ten feet, it lands on its back. Within seconds, the baby giraffe rolls to an upright position, with legs tucked under its body. As it takes in the world for the first time, mama stands over her newborn for about a minute. Then in a less-than-motherly manner, she swings her long pendulant leg and gives her baby a swift kick, sending it tumbling head over heels. When it doesn't get up, she repeats the process. Then she repeats it again. And again. The struggle to rise is Herculean. Finally, the calf stands for the first time. But "Mommy Dearest" isn't quite done. Walking over, she sweeps her leg soccer-style and kicks her baby's feet right out from under it once more!

Why in the world would a mother do something so bizarre and cruel to her newborn? It's a matter of simple survival. She knows that if her calf is to persevere in the wild, it must possess the ability to get up quickly and stay with the herd, where it finds safety. Packs of hyenas, leopards and lions lie in wait, ready to devour a baby giraffe. They'll quickly enjoy a feast if mom doesn't teach her calf to get moving from day one. What appears to be cruelty is actually an act of love.

Love doesn't always look like love; whether it's coming from a mama giraffe or our Lord. At times our Loving Father allows us to get kicked around a bit and knocked off our feet. But like the baby giraffe, our struggles are *always* for our benefit. Proverbs 3:12 states, "The Lord disciplines those He loves, as a father the son he delights in." Second Corinthians 4:17 informs us that "our light and momentary troubles are achieving for us an eternal glory." What feels like trouble, turns out to be triumph—"an eternal glory." As we struggle, let's keep our eyes on the prize.

Ever feel like God's got it in for you? Vanquish that thought immediately! God is *always* looking out for our best interest, but when we're in the midst of a good swift kick, it sure doesn't seem like it. Next time we feel kicked around, let's thank God and roll with the punches (or rather kicks). Anticipate greater times ahead, and remember some of our greatest blessings come disguised as kicks.

Principle: Some of life's greatest blessings come disguised as "kicks."

Promise: Our troubles are achieving for us an eternal glory.

Ponder:

- Are you currently experiencing some form of God's loving discipline?
- How can you grow from this experience to become more like God?

Prayer: *Loving Father, open my spiritual eyes to appreciate Your "kicks." Help me understand You always act in my best interest.*

Pursue: For a deeper dive, study Hebrews 12:1–13.

Perceptions: Record any ideas God puts on your heart from this devotion.

I CAN SEE!

I slowly awakened, blinking my eyelids as my vision adjusted to the grayish light. Suddenly, I jolted upright, shook my wife, and shouted, "Linda, I can see! I can see!" Opening her eyes, she gasped as well. "Yes! It's incredible! So can I!" Does anyone believe that actually happened? Of course not. For one simple reason. Both of us can already see each morning when we awaken. Viewing a majestic sunrise or my wife's beautiful face each morning truthfully isn't quite as significant as a bag of gold dropping from the sky, because it's the norm.

I do have a friend who's totally blind. He's never witnessed a sunrise or seen a baby's smile. How would he react if he woke up this morning and could see? Would it be a big deal? I would fully expect him to run around his house screaming, "I can see! I can see!"

How often do we fail to appreciate the simple blessings of life? Being able to see and hear. Having food to eat and an abode we call "home." The freedom to speak our minds and worship without fear of arrest. How many people on this planet would trade places with me? A blind billionaire would give away all his wealth for the gift of sight. Yet most of us who are blessed to see the world around us think little of it.

Please don't feel guilty. Feel grateful. The simple blessings of life are perhaps some of the greatest. Six times in Ecclesiastes, Solomon urges us to appreciate these simple blessings. "God wants all people to eat and drink and be happy in their work, which are gifts from God" (3:13 NCV). Food, drink, work. Add to that the companionship of a spouse (9:9). All simple blessings. Not the pursuit of wealth or fame or pleasure. Sure, I can enjoy the goodies of this world, if God blesses me with them (1 Timothy 6:17). But let's start by appreciating life's simple blessings.

Gratitude for life's simple blessings is an antidote to virtually every troubling mindset that afflicts us. Feeling anxious? Fearful? Stressed out? Pause for a moment. Focus on those simple blessings. We're buried up to our necks in amazing wealth and rarely consider it. Let's try that tomorrow morning as we awaken and view the early light. Feel free to shout out loud, "I can see!"

Principle: Gratitude is an antidote to a mindset of anxiety, stress, and fear.

Promise: Focusing on life's simple blessings frees me to enjoy life.

Ponder:

- What are some of the simple blessings of life God bestows on you each day? Take a moment and compose a list of them.
- How can you value these blessings in a greater way?

Prayer: *Loving Father, fill me with a grateful heart. Help me pursue life's simple blessings every day.*

Pursue: For a deeper dive, study Ecclesiastes 2:24–26 and 3:10–14.

Perceptions: Record any ideas God puts on your heart from this devotion.

GET OUT OF JAIL FREE?

For some folks, life is just one big game. Consider the case of a Minnesota man who was arrested for a felony warrant. He actually presented the deputy a "Get out of jail free" card from a Monopoly game! He quickly discovered that the card doesn't work in real life. He went straight to jail and did not "Pass Go." Bail was set at $5,000. "We appreciate the humor," the sheriff's office posted on Facebook. "A for effort!"

Perhaps we're more like this fellow than we care to admit. In the midst of our anxious times, all we want is an easy fix to our struggles. Push a button, problem solved. Flash a "Get out of jail free" card and everything's okay. Just get rid of my difficulties, Lord. "Hakuna matata." No worries, no troubles for the rest of my days.

But God wants so much more for us. His agenda is for me to become like Jesus. And He loves me enough to allow anxious situations to penetrate my precious little world, smashing my idols and teaching me to depend on Him. These struggles we wrestle to avoid are the fuel that propel us toward the image of Christ. In Philippians 3:8–10 Paul shares his goal in life: to "know

Christ," discarding the comforts of this world as "trash." Then he states he wishes to "share the in his sufferings and become like him in his death." How many of us would embrace that? Yet it's exactly what we sign on for as followers of Jesus.

Here's the underlying issue: my agenda and God's are vastly different. Most of us are addicted to comfort. We want *what* we want, *when* we want it, the *way* we want it. And if we don't get it...watch out! At times our level of entitlement can be thicker than frozen lard.

We work so hard to maintain our comfort. What if we surrendered our comfort and lived in a place of connection to Jesus? (John 15:5). We would experience a life far more fulfilling than chasing after comfort. We would know the joy of the Lord. We don't need to present a "Get out of jail free card" to our Father. He's already set us free. Let's be grateful for all He's done and center our lives on Him. He'll take care of the rest.

Principle: God allows us to experience anxious situations so we can become more like Jesus.

Promise: When we surrender our comfort, we experience a far more fulfilling life.

Ponder:

- How can you learn to surrender your comfort and live in a place of connection to Jesus?

- What step is God showing you to take today to "know Christ" more deeply?

Prayer: *Lord Jesus, I confess my tendency to desire a life of comfort. Take me to a higher level of living in connection with You, so I can experience more of Your joy.*

Pursue: For a deeper dive, study Philippians 3:1–11.

Perceptions: Record any ideas God puts on your heart from this devotion.

MONKEY BUSINESS

Imagine finding your phone you believed was lost, only to discover a video, as well as a number of "selfies" snapped by a monkey! For two days, twenty-year-old Zackrydz Rodzy, a Malaysian college student, searched in vain for his phone. Finally, he heard it ringing in his yard. After examining it, Rodzy realized a monkey had stolen it. He laughingly shared that the mischievous Macaque should create his own Instagram account since the camera abounds with humorous selfies, slow-motion videos, time-lapses, and portraits. "I was shocked. The suspect's face was plastered on the screen. It was hilarious," Zack said.

I'm not sure how much our simian friend understood about his actions. Perhaps his deeds were completely random, but it's possible he was imitating the behavior of humans around him. "Monkey see; monkey do" is more than a trivial maxim.

Regardless, the primate's behavior points toward a trend in our culture—obsession with self. What does the term "selfie" imply? Philippians 2:3–4 commands us, "Don't be selfish; don't try to impress others. Be humble, thinking of others as better than yourselves. Don't look out only for your own interests, but take an interest in others, too" (NLT). Well, that's about as easy as wrestling a phone from a monkey!

Want to be free? Truly free? Look to the example of the most unselfish servant ever to walk planet earth— Jesus. Shortly before He died, the Son of God washed His followers' stinking feet, for goodness sake! Putting others first lifts our heads above the muck and mire of self-obsession and propels us toward Christ-like concern for others.

Our preoccupation with self generates a downward spiral of insecurity, entitlement, and anxiety. The more self-absorbed we become, the harder we labor to maintain our image. "Will I get as many likes on this post as my last one?" Or, "How come she got more 'kissy lips' on her picture than I did?" During these times where many of us are stuck at home or singing the blues in a myriad of manners, isn't it worth pursuing a path of unselfish service? We'll discover joy like we've never known. Entitlement and victimhood will vanish faster than a stolen phone.

Maybe it's time we considered others' needs above our own. Maybe it's time we helped someone else before we take care of number one. Maybe it's time we live in gratitude, rather than entitlement. Otherwise, we're just "monkeying around."

Principle: Our culture is spiraling downward into self-obsession.

Promise: Serving others brings us joy like we've never known.

Ponder:

- In which of your relationships do you need improve your service?
- What specific steps can you take to accomplish this?

Prayer: *Jesus, thank You for showing us how to serve. Would You enable me through Your power to serve others as you did?*

Pursue: For a deeper dive, study Philippians 2:1–11.

Perceptions: Record any ideas God puts on your heart from this devotion.

AN UNPAYABLE DEBT

In the winter of 1777–78, George Washington's troops at Valley Forge were enduring brutal conditions as they trudged through the snow barefooted and half-starved. Washington appealed to wealthy merchant Jacob DeHaven for help. DeHaven responded by loaning the Continental Army $50,000 in gold and $400,000 in supplies. His generosity enabled the troops to survive the winter and ultimately win the Revolutionary War. However, the loan was never repaid.

In 1990 DeHaven's descendants sued the government to collect the delinquent debt. With compounded interest, they figured Uncle Sam owed them a whopping $141.6 billion. Needless to say, they lost the case and the appeal.

Aside from the descendants' greed, we're struck by the enormity of this debt. Some debts simply cannot be repaid. In a sense, all the money on earth couldn't repay DeHaven for his generosity. His loan was all that stood between the collapse of the Revolution and victory over the British. He saved the cause of freedom for America. An unpayable debt.

But consider this. The debt owed to DeHaven dwarfs in comparison to the price Jesus paid for our sins. Second Corinthians 5:21 states, "Christ had no sin, but God made him become sin so that in Christ we could be right with God" (ERV).

By His sacrifice, Jesus took upon himself our unpayable debt—the guilt of every sin ever committed. His cross is all that stands between eternal separation from God and unending bliss with Jesus. He paid our debt to set us free. No amount of money or good deeds could ever repay Him. We simply need to receive His gift.

Right now, we find ourselves in the throes of a spiritual Valley Forge. Our minds are overwhelmed with uncertainty about the future. But let's put life in perspective. Our eternal debt has been paid! Our future is secure. Our eternity is certain. In the blink of an eye, our struggles will be over and we will be with God. That's why Scripture describes our troubles as "light and momentary" (2 Corinthians 4:17). Compared to eternity, our present problems are miniscule. How much better could life get?

Unquestionably, God's gift of eternal life is the greatest blessing ever bestowed on mankind. All he asks is that we surrender our lives to Jesus. Then we can lift our eyes to heaven and thank Him for rescuing us from our unpayable debt.

Principle: Jesus saved us from our unpayable debt.

Promise: We have been made right with God through Jesus.

Ponder:

- How does knowing your eternal future is secure empower you to face the struggles of the present?
- Who do you know who needs to say yes to Jesus's offer of eternal life? How can you pray for them?

Prayer: *Jesus, there are no words to express how grateful I am that You paid my unpayable debt. I will thank You for all eternity.*

Pursue: For a deeper dive, study Psalm 103.

Perceptions: Record any ideas God puts on your heart from this devotion.

A BANQUET FROM HEAVEN

"Come to dinner!" my mother yelled. Stepping into the dining room, my senses were overwhelmed with the aroma of baked turkey. There, before my watering mouth, spread her Thanksgiving dinner. Turkey, dressing, gravy, mashed potatoes, sweet potato casserole, cranberry sauce, freshly-baked yeast rolls…a feast to delight the taste buds!

In Revelation 3:20 Jesus invites us to dine with Him in a spiritual feast. "Behold, I stand at the door and knock. If anyone hears my voice and opens the door, I will come in to him and eat with him, and he with me" (ESV). Jesus knocks at the door of each person's heart, calling us to open our lives to Him and experience the spiritual feast God has prepared for us. But opening my heart to Jesus isn't always easy. I must surrender my pride and acknowledge I need a Savior. I give up doing life my way. But the rewards we receive are so much greater than any sacrifices we make, they're not even worth comparing.

Picture this. A huge banquet table spread with our favorite foods, representing the spiritual blessings God offers. Jesus invites us to accept His invitation and dine with Him. Now imagine a dumpster containing stale food, characterizing the short-term pleasures this world offers: power, prestige, popularity, etc. We all face the choice of which "meal" we will consume.

Why on earth would we choose to dine on the spoiled food of this world, when we have a spiritual feast available? Because short-term spiritual "dumpster-diving" requires fewer sacrifices. But long-term? The food of this world turns moldy and stale, ultimately leading to destruction. But saying yes to Jesus opens our lives to what our hearts truly long for: love, freedom, and hope. This isn't a one-and-done event. We continue to make this choice each day of our lives.

As much as I delighted in my mother's Thanksgiving meal, God's spread is much more satisfying. He invites us to devour the dishes of eternal life, peace of mind, and purpose in life, as well as a host of other delicacies. All He asks is that we open the door of our hearts and trust in Him. And unlike my mother's Thanksgiving meal, Christ's feast continues to satisfy us for eternity.

Principle: God's spiritual banquet is far more fulfilling than anything the world offers.

Promise: When we open the door of our hearts to Jesus, He feasts with us.

Ponder:

- What "food" of this world most appeals to your flesh?
- What steps can you take to continually feast on the banquet that Jesus offers in your heart?

Prayer: *Lord Jesus, thank You for the spiritual banquet You have provided for me. I open the door of my heart to You and say yes to Your invitation.*

Pursue: For a deeper dive, study Isaiah 55.

Perceptions: Record any ideas God puts on your heart from this devotion.

AFTERWORD

We had pretty much given up hope. After twenty-eight years, our retail store, The Bird's Nest, was facing closure due to COVID-19. We were labeled "non-essential" and had shut down two months earlier. We decided to take one more shot before we permanently closed the doors.

We placed "essential items" near the entrance—hand-made masks, sanitizer, and (of course) toilet paper—items one wouldn't normally find in a boutique. With a tape measure stretched across the floor, I placed colored markers every six feet. Mother's Day weekend was typically a banner time for sales. On Friday we opened our doors, expecting to celebrate a day of soaring business. By 4:00 we had moved a whopping $5.00 in merchandise out the door.

Before leaving the next morning, we prayed. "Lord, we don't know the future, only You do. It appears we're going to have to shut down and probably leave California." Then in Gideon-like fashion, I added. "If You want us to stay open, please give us some kind of sign."

At 4:00 the cash register tape revealed $285 in sales, not even close to what we hoped for. We turned off the lights, and Linda climbed in our van. In despair, I was locking the store's front door. In the corner of my eye, I saw a blur. Running toward me, waving her arms, a middle-aged woman shouted, "Don't close! Don't close! I need to do some shopping!"

I motioned to Linda, and she came inside. Over the next several hours, this lady bought $4,000 in merchandise! The largest individual sale in twenty-eight years of business. If I had locked the door thirty seconds earlier, we would have missed her. Here's the kicker. We never saw her again. She left some large pieces of furniture she purchased. I called and texted numerous times. Eventually we sold them.

What are the odds? We pray for a sign, and God gives us the biggest single sale in our history—right at the moment we were closing. Clearly, we had our sign.

But God loves to show off. The next day, we encountered another customer. Through tear-filled eyes, she begged us to continue doing business, because she experienced so much love from our staff. The following day, another shopper shared, "This store saved my life." She lived across the street. When her son died in a motorcycle accident, she found refuge and healing by being able to share her burdens with our store's team.

From the beginning, The Bird's Nest's mission was to serve those in our community. But now the Lord had opened our eyes to just how much He wanted to work through us. We were invigorated with renewed purpose. From this point, sales increased, and now, five months later, our profits are back to pre-coronavirus days.

In the Preface I briefly mentioned how God had supernaturally saved our business. But we're not unique. God wants to do the same for all of us; maybe not in such a dramatic manner, but He always comes through, one way or the other. Regardless of our situation, God's in the middle of the mess. He *will* deliver us, sometimes in unexpected, unimagined ways. Trust Him. Wait on Him. He invariably enables us to *Thrive in Troubled Times.*

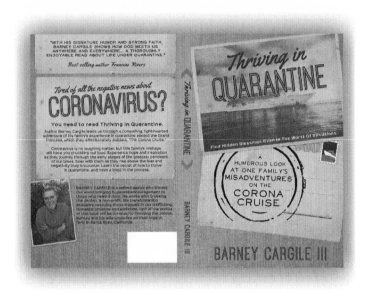

On sale at Amazon for $9.99

Barney Cargile's first book, *Thriving in Quarantine*, chronicles the misadventures of his family on the *Grand Princess*. After COVID-19 was discovered onboard, they were confined to their cabin for six days and at Travis Air Force Base for two weeks. Traveling with three small children, the phrase, "If anything can go wrong, it will," was more than a vague expression. You'll laugh out loud, even as they navigate through the greatest pandemic in modern times.

New York Times best-selling author Francine Rivers said this about *Thriving in Quarantine*: "With his signature humor and strong faith, Barney Cargile shows how God meets us anywhere and everywhere…a thoroughly enjoyable read about life under quarantine."

Made in the USA
Middletown, DE
24 March 2022